Playing 20 Questions With God

By
Jeff Eisen, Ph.D.

An Omnius Book

Published by Airleaf

www.omnians.com

ISBN: 1-60002-138-7

Cover art and figures by Ariel Eisen

Also by Jeff Eisen

Oneness Perceived. A Window into Enlightenment

Powertalk. How to Speak it, Think it, and Use it

Get the Right Job Now

"We have at our fingertips a means of accurately distinguishing truth from falsehood, workable from unworkable, benevolent from malign. We can illuminate the hidden forces, hitherto overlooked, that determine human behavior. We have a means of finding answers to previously unresolved personal and social problems at our disposal. Falsehood needn't hold sway over our lives any longer."

--- *David Hawkins* ---

"The beginning of freedom from the pain-body lies first of all in the realization that you *have* a pain-body. Then, more important, is your ability to stay present enough, alert enough, to notice the pain-body in yourself as a heavy influx of negative emotion when it becomes active. When it is recognized, it can no longer pretend to be you and live and renew itself through you.

It is your conscious Presence that breaks the identification with the pain-body. When you don't identify with it, the pain-body can no longer control your thinking and so cannot renew itself anymore by feeding on your thoughts. The pain body in most cases does not dissolve immediately, but once you have severed the link between it and your thinking, the pain-body begins to lose energy. Your thinking ceases to be clouded by emotion; your present perceptions are no longer distorted by the past. The energy that was trapped in the pain body then changes its vibrational frequency and is transmuted into Presence."

--- *Eckhart Tolle* ---

It appears that almost all people possess "paranormal" abilities... Not only can people communicate with the minds of all the people, but they can also communicate with other people's *bodies*. Reliable evidence is becoming available that the conscious mind of one person can produce repeatable and verifiable effects on the body of another... *In* the kind of alternative medicine known as spiritual healing... the healer acts upon the organism of his or her patient by "spiritual" means - that is, by sending a healing force or healing information. Healer and patient can be directly face-to-face, or miles apart; distance does not seem to affect the outcome. The effectiveness of this kind of healing may be surprising, but it is well documented. Renowned physician Larry Dossey calls the corresponding medical practice "era III nonlocal medicine,"

--- *Ervin Laszlo* ---

Foreword
By
Jeanie DeRousseau Eisen, Ph.D.

All my life I have been treated to words, phrases, and stories that "glow" in my inner space. Such is the case with Jeff's "conscious unlearning". It seems to be an entry into a broad and vast vista of consideration, a consideration that is bound to change my world.

Of course, I contrast it immediately to "learning", one of those golden idols of the modern world that guides us daily as we follow instruction manuals to operate our technology, set out to master some new exercise modality, and send our children to school. There seems to be no end to what we can learn.

But have you noticed lately a kind of overwhelm? A huge proportion of our kids are labeled attention-deficit, many of us routinely escape into television (which effectively quiets our thinking brain), thrill seeking (which does the same thing through focused attention), or drugs; and most of us are experiencing a sense of exhaustion rather than satisfaction at the end of the day. It almost feels as if there is no more room to learn about one more thing!

As a physical anthropologist I "learned" the very important role of learning in the evolution of humanity. Among all other species our big brains have given us the advantage of learning from our experiences in one lifetime, from our elders and our cultures, rather than learning the slow way through selective survival (only those survive who are genetically inclined toward certain behaviors, advantageous in a given environment).

Interestingly, I also "learned" that for this reason, evolution has slowed, maybe even stopped in the human species. It has done this especially in the western world, because we have developed sophisticated technologies and methods that keep alive people that would normally be weeded out by natural selection. There is some selection (read evolution) still going on in the parts of the third world where disease and malnutrition rage, but presumably that is not about to change the nature of our species, although it may be affecting the frequencies of certain genes.

But I wonder if the line of traditional anthropology is correct. Has technology indeed become a buffer between evolutionary pressures and us, or has technology and what we have learned actually become the pressure that is moving us forward on our evolutionary path? Perhaps both?

Enter Jeff and "conscious unlearning".

In this book Jeff proposes that there are things we learn that are actually *not* serving us, but that *evolution has not provided us with a mechanism to unlearn these habits.* In some sense this would be proposing that too much evolution has occurred, our learning has gotten "too efficient", and we find ourselves not being served by what we know. We're like the buck, grown so successful in competing for females by growing huge antlers, that now his antlers threaten his own survival.

Jeff tells a famous Buddhist story about a student who comes to a Master and wants to learn from him. The Master declines, then sits him down to tea and begins to pour tea into a cup. He keeps pouring until the potential student cries, "Stop, Master. The cup is full. No more will go in." At which time the Master looks him in the eye and agrees, "Exactly."

It seems we are that student at the table of the Master. We are embedded in a system full of information to learn; yet, unless we are one of the lucky few, the system and the information has little meaning for us. It will not go in.

Part of the problem, perhaps the major part, is what Jeff discusses here. Our internal thoughts and concerns occupy our inner space so fully that learning something new becomes a problem. Seeing something afresh, accessing a "beginner's mind", becomes an impossibility.

As Jeff sees it, the conclusions of a lifetime are firmly embedded in our unconscious body/mind, continuously interpreting our present experience, and leaving no room for something different and more real to emerge. Since just about everyone around us is also "full" of their own conclusions, "full" of their own interpretations and perspectives, one may begin to understand why husbands and wives can't understand one another, bosses and workers can't relate to one another, and heads of state can't come to any real agreement.

What Jeff and I have lived, what Jeff is sharing here, is a route into making the space we need to fill our tea cup with something different. If we unlearn what no longer serves us (that tea of self-consciousness that guides most of human behavior today), we will be consciously making the space for our own growth into a better and more appropriate relationship with one another. If many of us do this, we will be opening a way for something new to emerge in the network of humanity that we are.

In this sense, I believe that "conscious unlearning" is no less than an evolutionary advance that requires our collective, conscious participation. It is driven by the intense internal pressure that we experience as we try to relate to a world that, at the least, is changing at lightning speed, and at the worst, appears to have gone mad. It may even be that our continued success as a species depends on each of us making a conscious decision to release enough of our unconscious biases that we may relate to each other in new and inclusive ways.

So please enter here. "Learn" how to "unlearn", how to consciously take charge of your inner space, and how to change the world from the inside out. For as Einstein said, "Problems cannot be solved at the same level of consciousness that created them." *It seems we must decide, one by one, to change our inner worlds, our self-conscious points of view, if we are to change what it looks like out there before it's too late.*

Imagine continuing the 3.5 billion year evolution of life on earth by consciously making peace within ourselves, a spacious opening to wisdom, so that we know how to proceed in our relationships, both personal and collective. Imagine if we and the world began to behave from an authentic clarity, relating to one another without self-consciousness, resting firmly in the present moment and able to cocreate solutions to all our problems. Imagine... and decide...

"Never underestimate what a small number of people can do to change the world. Indeed, it is the only thing that ever has." *Margaret Mead, anthropologist*

Preface

This book describes a path of self-repair, self-empowerment, and ultimately, self-transformation. Along this path all sorts of abilities and accomplishments open up, ones that become extraordinary aids to the attainment of health, serenity, prosperity, and spiritual growth. I have named this inner exploration and empowerment, PsychoNoetics, or the Clearing Path.

PsychoNoetics is an intrapsychic and energetic process. It does not work via the ordinary channels of the material world. You don't have to take any drugs, make physical contact, or do any physical exercises. Furthermore, any dialogue is only to focus on what needs to be let go of; the actual letting go takes place intentionally and unconsciously, in the psychonoetic dimension, the dimension of quantum consciousness. PsychoNoetics rests on miracles, but they are ordinary miracles, as ordinary as *intending* to express a thought and having the right words come out of your mouth.

My journey into PsychoNoetics rested on developing two intrapsychic abilities: the first was intuitive diagnosis (through the process of auto-kinesiological testing); the second was intentional clearing. I have come to refer to these as psychonoetic testing and clearing. I firmly believe that these two supposedly paranormal abilities are, in fact, normal and within everybody's grasp.

However, mastering these abilities was not mastering my computer. Mastering PsychoNoetics entailed elevating my consciousness, and that called for a little work and a big leap of faith. However, every clearing stretched my awareness, so that my consciousness transformed as my skill and understanding of PsychoNoetics deepened.

Self-transformation is a journey we all are on together. We take different side roads on this journey, only to come back, share notes and draw maps for one another. Some of the people on the journey we know personally, some are so famous that we have heard about them, but most we are completely unaware of. It doesn't matter because in some way they are all us, we are all them, and all of us are part of something bigger.

We have not completed our journey. Perhaps we will never complete it in this lifetime. Perhaps it will have to wait for our next lifetime or somebody else's lifetime. I suspect there is no difference, except, of course, from our individual points of view. Maybe some wise and valiant souls have completed it already. Or maybe there is no completion, only the next bend in the road unfolding the next vista.

This book is a travel guide to some of the territory I have explored in my spiritual inquiry and personal life. Then, and only then, has it informed my practice as a psychotherapist and a spiritual teacher.

Where I am ahead of you, use me as a guide. Where you are abreast of me, walk alongside. Where you are ahead, lead the way.

About the Format of this Book

Book I. *The Understanding Unfolds* consists of two parts: my personal story of how PsychoNoetics evolved, and a presentation of foundational ideas. The chapters are interleaved; presentation and story alternate to keep pace with one another. **My story is set in italics**, and, I believe, offers a valuable window into how personal experience and cognitive insights are one organic process.

The other chapters (set in conventional typeface) are my current conclusions about what PsychoNoetics is, what it can do for each of us, and how it fits into the worlds of science and spirituality. By the interleaving of my story and conclusions, I mean to clearly convey the evolution of my ideas.

Book II. *The PsychoNoetics Manual* is complete and explanatory in itself and can be used as a stand-alone book within a book. If you already know what PsychoNoetics is, or if you feel you've read enough of the introduction, backgrounds and principles, and you are anxious to get started, you can turn right to the manual and start using it.

Book III. *An Evolutionary Psychology for an Evolving World* goes deeper into the principles of PsychoNoetics, offers a theory of mind which integrates the physical and the psychological realms around the defense of identity, and talks about allergies, illnesses, stress, and "psychological" disorders in that unified context. Then, it goes on to place that content in an even wider, evolutionary context. It is a very important section that breaks new ground in the synthesis of psychology and consciousness.

PsychoNoetics, the word

The word *PsychoNoetics* is derived from two words. The first is psychology, the science of behavior and the brain/mind. The second is noetics, the science of consciousness. So

PsychoNoetics refers to that science of mind and behavior that is based not on an examination of the physical brain/mind, but of the field of consciousness (as it can be accessed by human awareness). I call that field the psychonoetic field.

Acknowledgments

This book is a family affair. Though I have crystallized the understanding and practices of PsychoNoetics, my wife Jeanie and daughter Ariel are integral parts of my story, and have each contributed to the book as well. Gratitude is too small a word for how I feel about them.

Table of Contents

Discovering PsychoNoetics, the story
Part 1. I die to who I was

This story begins in New York City on Christmas Eve, 1984, the night my life ended. It happened very fast — and it happened like this. I was walking on a dark street on the upper eastside of Manhattan, on my way to a Christmas party at my sister's house, when I noticed that squeaking sounds were coming out of my mouth. Seconds later I started to lose control of my body and in my last, desperate remnant of consciousness before blacking out, I knew that I was dying.

I came to, being lifted onto a stretcher. On the way to the hospital, the ambulance attendant explained to me that a bystander had observed me convulsing. I had had a seizure.

The next three months or so were taken up with trying to find out why I had had a seizure. My neurologist attributed it the selenium I had been taking to control my allergies. A naturopathic physician I consulted attributed to it to my inorganic diet. And a fellow psychologist attributed it to the stress of my recent divorce. This wild and free period of speculation was arrested by the event of a second seizure, which was followed by a series of more probing tests, including a second CAT scan.

The CAT scan revealed a large, shadowy mass, which was thought to be an area of bleeding on the first CAT scan. Now the real diagnosis descended like a dark cloud over my life...a meningioma, a non-malignant tumor of the meninges, the outer covering of the brain...in short, I had a brain tumor.

Well, the good news was that it was not cancer, and it was on the surface of the brain, not deep inside; so, theoretically at least, it was operable. The bad news, however, was that it was very large and clinging to my brain, rather than nicely separated. More to the point, it was clinging in areas that were responsible for many higher functions, including speech.

So, although it was operable, sort of, my surgeon wanted to try a less invasive approach first. This less invasive approach was plenty invasive in its own right. It consisted of threading a catheter through an artery in my groin until it reached the blood supply of the meningioma, at which time a gobbet of crazy glue was shot through it. The idea was to embolize the blood supply to the tumor, so that it would die and be absorbed by my body.

The procedure was only half successful. It did embolize the tumor, but unfortunately, not completely. And as we followed its progress over the following weeks, the blood supply started to come back. So we would have to operate after all. Dr. Ranserhoff would supply the operation; I would supply the tumor. In the meantime, there was also an unfortunate side effect. The blood supply to the nerves controlling my face was successfully embolized, and the left side of my face became paralyzed. It would probably come back, sort of. But in the meantime, I had to sleep with my eye taped shut, so that it wouldn't dry out.

Power Talk and my career
I was operated on in the early spring, right before my book <u>Power Talk</u> *was published. I went into the operation afraid, and I came out*

with my fears realized. My right arm and leg were paralyzed, and I was utterly unable to speak.

Power Talk caught on instantly, particularly with women, and excerpts appeared in all the women's magazines. Simon & Schuster wanted to put me on the road for a publicity tour. There was only one difficulty, me. I couldn't smile. I couldn't shake hands, and I couldn't speak.

I was also terrorized. While formerly I was a confident, almost cocky guy, I had become ridden with anxiety. I had lost trust in my body. Although I was walking almost normally, my speech was gradually returning, and I was even regaining use of my right arm and some crude functioning in my hand, I was always afraid of having another seizure. This anxiety was partly psychological and partly neurological. When I expected any degree of performance from myself, it precipitated an anxiety attack that would render me almost completely unable to speak.

I had to give up both teaching and my psychoanalytic practice. I just couldn't function. My world collapsed into my family, i.e., my mother and sister, and my girlfriend Debbie. While Debbie stood by me, it was extremely hard for both of us. She was used to my making the decisions. When she had to take the lead, things became very stressful for her. Also, she had been attracted to me because of my strength and confidence, and when I lost that, she lost her respect for me and hence her attraction. After about a year, when I was more or less able to live alone, we separated.

If you think you have your life together, both psychologically and spiritually, and want to put it to the test, try what I did. Get a brain tumor with all the trimmings and tell me how you come out. I would be interested to know.

Before my first seizure I was well on my way to becoming an authority on matters both psychological and spiritual. I had a Ph.D. and was a trained psychoanalyst and psychosynthesist. I had students, I had clients, and I wrote books. People listened to me. I even listened to myself. Now a little bit of adversity had come into my life – well, perhaps not so little - and everything collapsed, not only my outer life, but my inner as well. I became demoralized, despairing and depressed. My life as a man, a therapist, and spiritual authority was over. I had come from living fully to just existing and had discovered that great American occupation – hopelessly killing time.

There are a lot of stories out there about people who have been moved to a spiritual realization through sickness and adversity. This is not one of those stories. Any little measure of spiritual progress I had made in my life was lost when I got sick. However, time does heal, and in time my ordinary abilities to walk, talk, and chew gum returned, although perhaps not simultaneously. What didn't return, at least not then, was my self-confidence, my verve and, most of all, – my spiritual connection. Life had become all about fear and survival. I had entered the dark night of the soul.

I climb my way back to "normalcy"

Gradually, my life became more normal. However, it was not the normalcy that I was used to. It was a kind of stepped-down normalcy, in which I wandered about the city amusing myself, but not really progressing in my life. Not teaching, not seeing clients, not writing.

Finally, I did something to change my life. I went to Miami and bought a sailboat, one big enough for me to live-aboard. Actually, this was not the first time I had visited Miami. The first time was about six months after the operation when I went down with Debbie to recuperate in a kinder climate. We rented a little apartment in Key Biscayne. While there, I had seen a 41-foot sloop for sale at a cheap price, and on a whim made a ridiculously low ball offer. I had forgotten all about it when, out of the blue, months later, I got a phone call in New York that my offer had been accepted. Five days later I was at Key Biscayne sleeping on my new yacht.

Jeanie and Oneness Perceived

The next thing to get me out of the postoperative doldrums was meeting Jeanie, the woman who was to become my wife. There was

4

something about Jeanie, some combination of emotional presence and vulnerability, that touched my soul, and brought out the healer in me that had gone dormant in the years AO (after operation).

It was co-dependency at first sight.   Jeanie found in me the personal psychotherapist that all of us think should be our due in life, while I clutched at Jeanie's sweet, accepting nature as if she was a lifeline thrown from God. It was a disastrous combination from the get go.

Within months I was proposing, and Jeanie was running away. The problem was not only did I want Jeanie to marry me; I also wanted her to give up her tenured position as Associate Professor of Anthropology at New York University and move to Miami with me. Some chutzpah for someone in my shoes...

But somehow, as Jeanie says, "our destiny was sealed", and our relationship grew into marriage and parenthood. Jeanie moved to Miami with me, our daughter Ariel was born there, and we continued the hero's journey, each of us wielding both "our stuff" and our good intentions. [For our wedding, Jeanie wrote me a song, "Who is this stranger I've known forever?" and I wrote her a poem, "Jeanie, ever cheery, ever teary".]

The "stuff" we were up against looked something like this. I was paranoid, perpetually frustrated, demanding, and distrustful. I was deeply afraid of losing Jeanie to motherhood the way I had lost my last wife, and Jeanie was my lifeline to normalcy! Jeanie, on the other hand, was a pleaser who was married to a man she couldn't please. She found herself increasingly overwhelmed by the reality of simultaneously meeting my needs and the needs of a baby, trying to stay connected to her profession, and feeling like a failure.

Despite the co-dependency dance, an intellectual and spiritual kinship grew between us. This took the form of a deepening dialogue, a questing to understand the nature of spirit and reality in all of its guises. That dialogue fanned the embers of my spiritual life and got me to asking the big questions once again. One sultry, Miami night I put this question to myself...“what is duality?” Almost immediately, I got the answer...“duality is Oneness perceived!”

Although this answer seemed obvious, it also seemed to have great portent, and I immediately started to make some notes. Over the period of the next 10 years or so, these notes grew into the book <u>Oneness Perceived: A Window into Enlightenment</u>, which was published by Paragon House in 2002. Oneness Perceived was one half of my spiritual journey. It was a chronicle of inquiry that took me into a deep understanding of enlightenment.

The other half of my spiritual journey has been my relationship with Jeanie. Although we came together, almost casually, out of mutual and dimly understood personal needs, there gradually emerged and is still emerging, a deeper movement, a deeper significance. I don't know whether it came out of some accidental combination of our personal needs and gifts, or as Jeanie would put it, the universe had a plan for us and put us together for one another's enlightenment. But I do know that the combination of our essential incompatibility and our love for one another kept us trying to work things out. It provided the impetus for the hard psychological and spiritual work that enlightenment requires.

By enlightenment, I don't mean the old, ivory tower kind of enlightenment, only sustainable by withdrawing from the world. I mean the kind of in your face, every day, here and now, fully committed to this life ordinary enlightenment; the kind of enlightenment that strives to live an ordinary life in an extraordinary way, full of love and honesty, nonreactive and nonpositional.

PsychoNoetics

*Out of the streams of my life I have formulated the **Clearing Path** of **PsychoNoetics™**, the transformational, healing technology that I'm presenting in this book. My relationship with Jeanie is one of these streams. Without Jeanie I don't think I would have developed the Clearing Path, and without the Clearing Path I don't think I would be* *nearly the person I am today. And I don't think Jeanie and I would still be together.*

PsychoNoetics is a way of letting go of those positions or identities that all of us hold, both in our bodies and in our psyches. The technique can be applied to the entire gamut of identities from the allergic identities of the immune system to the emotional identities of the ego. PsychoNoetics has improved my physical health to the point where I can function almost normally in every aspect of my life and has improved my psychological health to the point where I can resume what seems to be my true destiny as a psychological healer and a spiritual teacher.

This book, the second book of my new life, is an introduction to PsychoNoetics. I offer it to you with the hopes that it will open the door to your self-transformation, as it did to mine. It will be followed by a third book, already being written, which will go even more deeply into the nature of enlightenment and the practice of PsychoNoetics as a transformational discipline.

To be continued...

Chapter 1
God, Healing, and the Nature of Reality

What if we had a hotline to God so that we could ask Him any question and He would answer it immediately? I'm here to tell you that it's possible, but there are three conditions that have to be met. First, the question has to be about something real, not something that is imaginary or arbitrary, not just an idea. Second, it has to concern something that exists now, in the eternal present, not the past or future. And third, we have to know how to ask the question - and of course, how to understand the answer. In a way, we have to play a game of 20 Questions[1] with God.

---

[1] Twenty Questions, for those of you who haven't played this game incessantly on long extended car trips, is a word game that starts when someone says the words "I'm thinking of something..." The listeners in turn ask, "Is it animal, vegetable, or mineral?" in an effort to hone in on what the speaker is thinking of. After the listeners receive the answer to this question, they can ask exactly 20 more questions, but only questions that can be answered with a yes or a no. Although 20 questions is the limit, there is frequently a determination to stay with the process until the knowing is complete!

But there's more. Not only can we ask God questions and get *yes or no* answers, as in the game of 20 Questions; we can also ask for help in alleviating any problem. How can we use our connection with God to help us alleviate problems? We can do it in a very specific way, one that is not generally understood. We can use our connection to help us *unlearn*, which, of course, includes *identifying* that which we have to unlearn.

Learning and unlearning

Learning is, of course, usually a very efficient and beneficial process. In fact, if we couldn't both learn from the past and *integrate* what we had learned, we would have to learn everything in the present and continually relearn it. Every skill, from how to peel a banana to how to talk, would have to be relearned every time we needed it, and this would be not only inefficient, but also impossible. We need normal learning. It is essential for functioning.

However, what if there are lessons that we learned in the past that simply are *not* correct and have to be corrected? This happens frequently either because what we learned was mistaken in the first place or because the learning has ceased to be valid. Things have changed - changed enough so that what was once useful and true, is useful and true no longer. When such lessons in the past continue to guide our perceptions and behaviors into the future, suffering and dysfunction generally ensue.

In fact, over the last 20 years I have learned that the vast preponderance of our emotional and even physical problems emerge because we do not yet know how to unlearn the mistaken or no-longer-valid conclusions we have drawn from our past experiences. These conclusions, held fast in our memory, mislead us as they continually offer us references from the past that are invalid.

When we are unconsciously applying these misleading lessons, so that our perceptions of the present are distorted, we refer to it, among other things, *as being in memory*. And when we are in memory, we need to get out of it again, to come back wholly to the present. The only way to get out of memory that really works, is to *unlearn* the lessons we have learned. This frees our minds to perceive from a fresh place, and to learn anew from the vantage point of our greater, adult wisdom. But, amazingly, human evolution has developed no mechanism for *unlearning*.

Evolution does not go back, it just goes forward.

PsychoNoetics is a new field of understanding and technology that empowers each of us to take responsibility for *unlearning* whatever conclusions we hold that are no longer serving us. Prior to PsychoNoetics, and to some extent, a handful of other clearing modalities, there was really no way of unlearning a lesson once it was learned. The best we could do was to overlay our incorrect lessons and override our incorrect responses.

PsychoNoetics, however, is an evolutionary advance that allows us to *identify and unlearn* our incorrect lessons, and to do so instantly and permanently. The way entails using our connection with God level of being, and it's both simple and miraculous!

The difference between unlearning and forgetting

But before I continue, let me clarify the difference between unlearning and forgetting, which is, in turn, built upon the difference between information and assimilation. Information comes in the form of facts or knowing about. It really doesn't have much to do with us. Assimilation however, is when we make that which we learn a part of us. It is knowing by being.

Information is more or less conscious and is held in the mind. It can be easily forgotten and when it is forgotten it is gone. Assimilation, however, is unconscious. It is learning about ourselves in relationship to the outside world, and it becomes part of our being. Our conscious mind can forget about it, but it remains part of what we are. It becomes and remains part of our *identity*, and that cannot be forgotten. It can only be disidentified with or cleared.

So forgetting is different from unlearning or clearing. We can easily forget, but in order to unlearn, to clear the unconscious mind, to deconstruct an identity, we have to intend to do so, and follow a conscious process like PsychoNoetics, which uses our connection with God being.

Could God be consciousness?

When we encounter the word *God*, we have to ask ourselves what is being referred to. There have been almost as many interpretations of God as there are religions and spiritual traditions. But in the joining of spirit, psychology, and quantum physics, a new level of understanding of God is arising and supplanting the more traditional ones. In this understanding, God is sometimes seen as an all-encompassing, natural principal, something like the way the unified field works.

My understanding is even simpler than that. I work on the assumption that God is nothing more and nothing less than consciousness itself. In some ways, God is nothing other than our consciousness, that alive awareness that notices and experiences our lives.

However, the realization that our consciousness is God, is one that is usually lost to us. We lose touch with this realization because it is obscured by ideas and experiences of ourselves, limiting ones. So even though we all experience this consciousness, most of us don't realize what it is and therefore, who we are. We don't realize that we are God embodied, God in a body.

As an agnostic scientist, lately come to cautious belief, this explanation does not merely make sense; it is the only one that makes sense. As a matter of fact, coming to the realizations that not only is God consciousness, but also that we are indivisible with this consciousness, *allows* me to believe. It is the simplest formulation. It is also the formulation that lets me attribute to God all of the vastness, omnipotence, and mystery that all the prophets and mystics throughout time have attributed to Him (without doing violence to my rigorous, scientific mind), because to the best of my scientific understanding, consciousness alone fills that bill.

This, of course, means that God is the reality of who we really are. But if God is that, where does that leave the everyday reality of ourselves as separate, vulnerable, physical beings? Can that also be God? Even more to the point, where does it leave the ordinary reality of science, of classical physics, of cause and effect, of material things located in space and time interacting according to the laws of nature? For that matter, where does it leave the hard reality of economics and survival? Can these also be God?

My answer to these questions is that God is the reality of who we really are, but this is not ordinary reality. Ordinary reality is just the appearance of things. It is the way we perceive and conceive things, through our senses and our mind. Real reality is seeing through this *illusion of ourselves* as separate, physical things competing with other separate things in a world of separate things. It is also a seeing through the *illusion of perception*, which presents us with a world of separate things interacting with each other according to the laws of classical physics.

With that seeing through, we come to a quantum view of reality as a consciousness-like, simultaneous, non-local field. With this there emerges a deeper understanding of the reality of both God and ourselves. This, in turn, opens us to *the power of what we are*!

Working with our identities

There are all sorts of lessons, from how to tie our shoes to how to drive a car, which we learn in the past and bring to our present. But there is one, great class of lessons that stands above all others in guiding us. These are the *conclusions* we have formed about *who we are*. These conclusions become our *identities,* and our identities, in turn, form our reality. Our identities guide our perceptions, and our perceptions form our reality.

PsychoNoetics is a method of getting out of memory by identifying and unlearning incorrect lessons. But because lessons about ourselves aggregate into identities, PsychoNoetics also becomes a way of pinpointing, deconstructing, and *unlearning* our identities when it is appropriate to do so.

True identities and false ones

When is it appropriate to deconstruct an identity? When the identity is false, of course! When our identities are true, they are a reliable guide to perception, and of course, action. But, unfortunately, most people's identities are false, and false identities are responsible for the lion's share of the pain and suffering, both physical and psychological, that we experience in our lives.

What are false and true identities? This is a complex subject that will become clearer as we read on. For now, let's begin by saying that a false identity is one that is based upon false self-concepts, whereas our true identity is not conceptual at all, but rather is rooted in a greater reality, the reality that I have touched on in the preceding sections on God, reality, and consciousness.

In this book, I offer you a great gift, which has been given to me as well. It is the gift of *conscious unlearning*, the knowledge of how to heal and transform oneself by releasing false identities and relaxing into true ones. If you want to receive this gift, however, you're going to have to make a receptive field of yourself, and work in a different dimension of reality, one that the Western world has only begun to validate. This dimension is a joining of spirit and science, of God and reality, into a higher truth.

But, I assure you, that as you intend to receive, as you learn and practice PsychoNoetics, your thinking will open easily to this new paradigm.

Radical sanity

This brings us to the deepest level of this book, which is spiritual awakening, or what I sometimes call radical sanity. When we perceive the present from the viewpoint of the past, when we are in the grips of a false identity, when we are in memory, we are suffering from a delusion - and this delusion causes suffering. As we let go of all this, our natural beingness emerges, and we come to rest in the reality of our true nature, the reality of who we really are. Being in this reality is *radical sanity*, and radical sanity will open the doors to that compassionate clarity which is the highest state of human consciousness.

The mystery

How does our communication with God being work? Ultimately, it is a mystery, but in the final analysis, do we know how we do anything at all? Do we know how we walk, how we talk, how we eat, or even how we think? It's all a mystery! We just do it. We *form the intention,* and it happens. That is the way the techniques in this book work, and they are just as miraculous as God's works of nature, and just as ordinary as walking and talking. Knowing the power of our ordinary intentions, and how to harness them, is power indeed!

Discovering PsychoNoetics, the story
Part 2. Allergies open the door

The plot line continues in Seattle in the fall of 1995, when I first consulted an NAET (Nambudripad's Allergy Elimination Technique) practitioner. The relevant flashback, however, takes place more than 40 years before that, in 1953 on Fire Island, a beach resort on Long Island, N.Y., when I was thirteen and first developed hay fever.

One August morning I woke up sneezing and continued sneezing until October. It got so bad that every time I sneezed, I got a nosebleed. I had to stop swimming because when I went into the ocean, my nose would start bleeding again. That was the first time I was diagnosed as having allergies, hay fever, or allergic rhinitis, as Dr. Schwartz called it. He prescribed antihistamines and vitamins (C and B complex). He was very progressive for 1953. From then on it was official. I was an allergic child.

Much earlier, when I was still a small boy, our family doctor was my mother's cousin, Morris Blum. He was one of those warm, old-fashioned doctors that still made house calls, all bedside manner, reassurances and misdiagnoses. If he knew I had allergies, he didn't let on. Maybe they were unknown to medical science in the mid 40's. What he did do was to recommend to my parents that my tonsils be taken out, and while they were at it, they might as well take out my adenoids and anything else in the area, just to be safe. This, of course, did as much to help my allergies as a haircut, but I did hemorrhage on the gurney being wheeled from the operating room and had to be rushed inside again to save my life.

These were my earliest memories of what I now know to have been my allergies, but the oral history in my family goes back further still. I was a problem eater. My mother couldn't get me to eat a good meal. This is one story she was fond of telling…We were at Chester's resort in Pennsylvania. My reluctance to eat was getting to be a problem so my father, not usually there when I was being fed, he being at work, took over.   His paternal authority succeeded where my mother's maternal wheedling had failed. Trembling, I cleaned my plate. I can just imagine the scene…he full of pride…see how easy it is and trying not to gloat; she, battle-scarred veteran of a thousand food wars, wanting to kill us both. Then, I furnish one of the high points in her life, her vindication as a mother and a competent human being. I projectile vomit my father's triumph into his lap and all over the Chester's dining room. Her interpretation of this mirrored the pop-Freudian wisdom of the time, that eating was my battleground for autonomy. My simpler version today…food allergy!

Scroll forward to 1995 in Seattle. At 55 I was a card-carrying allergic, very sensitive to dairy, all grains, all legumes, and a scattering of everything else. I was also allergic to pollens, mildew, air pollution, chemical fumes, and cats, and was developing new allergies constantly. My symptoms, in no particular order, included stiffness, bloating, bowel disturbances, memory and concentration difficulties, fatigue, irritability, sinus problems, itchy eyes and palette, bronchial wheezing and more recently, tinnitus (ringing in my ears, probably sensitized by my surgery). All my life allergies had increasingly constricted my life, what I did, where I lived, and above all what I ate. After my surgery they became almost intolerable.

When I moved to Miami seven years earlier to recuperate, it had seemed like a good place about to become a better one. The city had a vibrancy about it, the climate and warm water had been gentle with my newly traumatized body, and I had escaped New York's pollution and pollens for awhile. Eventually, Miami became a jet set destination, not so wholesome a place for raising our daughter, and Florida's pollutants and pollens caught up with me.

In the summer of 1995, having just sold our house, we decided to try living in Seattle, a vacation spot we had fallen in love with two years earlier. We packed up the van and drove cross-country even though warned about the moldy Northwest. Allergies be damned.

Seattle

I was troubled by my usual allergies from the first, pollen, air pollutants, my favorite foods and, of course **mold spores** - of which Seattle was the number one producer in the nation! In September we moved from a house near Elliot Bay to one further inland. There was something about either the house or the location that amplified my tinnitus, from a background whine into a screaming presence impossible to ignore. As the rains increased, my tinnitus and all my allergies got steadily worse, until I could hardly bear one more second in the evergreen city.

Sometime in November Jeanie found a little display ad in an alternative health newsletter. It advertised an alternative cure for allergies. I wasn't open. Allergies were antibody reactions, some were even genetically determined, and I couldn't see how a little energy work could make much of a dent in them. However, Jeanie had one of her intuitions, so more to please her than anything else, I went along.

We found ourselves in the scantily furnished offices of what looked like a slightly overage surfer with the unreassuring name of Brightheart, Richard Brightheart. I was underwhelmed.

What happened next was even less convincing. One by one he placed little vials of clear fluid that had labels like egg mix, calcium, and vitamin C into our hands and then pushed down on our *outstretched arms to feel whether holding any particular vial weakened our muscles.   The vials looked like water, but I assumed they were dilute solutions of allergens.   Much later I found out that they were indeed water, which had, however, been zapped with the "energy signature" of the substance it was representing, using a weird machine (glowing tubes emitting sparks and Dr. Frankenstein rubbing his hands and giggling insanely in the background, that sort of thing would later come to mind).   Fortunately, I didn't know that at the time.*

The technique of kinesiology or muscle testing was familiar to me. I had gone to an acupuncturist named Russell Rogg in Miami the year before who had touched what are called alarm points on my body, supposedly corresponding to specific organs, while jacking my arm up and down like the handle of an old fashioned pump.   From this five minute procedure he gave me a diagnostic profile that, whatever its validity, could not be duplicated in thoroughness by a month of testing at the Mayo clinic at the cost of thousands of dollars and hundreds of syringes of my reluctantly given blood.   Amazingly, I got good results at Russell's hands, so I was not turned off by this aspect of Rich's technique.

The other stuff seemed strictly voodoo, but there was something in Rich's manner, some inner authority that kept me coming back.   He checked us, me, Jeanie, and Ariel, our daughter, six years old at the time, on a series of potential allergens called the 13 basics (Egg mix, Calcium, Vitamin C mix, B Complex mix, Sugar mix, Iron mix, Vitamin A mix, Mineral mix, Salt mix, Chlorides, Artificial sweeteners, Corn mix and Grain mix) and found me allergic to 8 of them.   Now I knew I was allergic to a lot of stuff, but I never suspected such unlikely offenders as calcium, iron and of all things salt.   How can you be allergic to salt!   Furthermore, I knew I wasn't allergic to eggs, because every time I eat something I'm allergic to my stomach swells up, and eggs, although I am not particularly fond of them were something I could eat freely.   However, muscles cannot tell a lie, or so the theory goes.

Twelve treatments and some hundreds of dollars later I was pronounced clear of these eight basic allergens that I still strongly suspected I was not allergic to in the first place: a triumph for energy medicine? Was I feeling any better? Not dramatically. What kept me coming back? The promise that were I to go on with the treatments I would eventually get to enjoy a cappuccino with a pan au chocolate, unbothered by my allergies to coffee, milk, chocolate and wheat. I'm a man of simple ambitions.

There was, however, also something that happened to Jeanie when she had just been treated that spurred me on as well. Part of the protocol of the treatment is avoidance of the treated allergen for 24 hours. Jeanie was avoiding chicken that particular day, but Ariel and I were not. Being the dutiful Mom, she opened up the roast chicken from the supermarket for us, and as she did, the wafting steam hit her face and she almost passed out from a reaction to the chicken smell. Her treatment had to be repeated, but we had learned that some adjustment was indeed occurring with our treatments, and we better pay close attention!

Allergies and energy systems

Let me talk a little more about allergies. When you get through this book, your picture of the human mind/body, allergies, the unconscious and all human possibilities might have changed considerably. So this section is going to include both what I learned from Rich and what I figured out later, since I cannot remember which came when.

First of all, the technique Rich practiced is known as Nambudripad's Allergy Elimination Technique, a.k.a. NAET. A very smart Indian lady, Devi Nambudripad, who is a chiropractor and an acupuncturist, and was a sufferer from allergies, developed it. Her story in a nutshell was that she took one bite of a carrot and got deathly ill. Her husband, also an acupuncturist, revived her with the needles. She fell asleep and when she came to she was still clutching the carrot. For some reason she not only felt fine, but also had

21

overcome her allergy to carrots. She put two and two together, "put it through a horn", and NAET was born.

Allergy can be defined as a normal, physical rejection that becomes exaggerated. When the nose begins to drip and the hay fever victim sneezes, this is an effort on the part of these organs to eliminate some of the irritants, such as pollen, causing the irritation. According to Dr. Nambudripad and oriental medicine in general (acupuncturists are Doctors of Oriental Medicine), the body is an energy system. There are pathways through which energy circulates called meridians. These meridians furnish energy to the major organs and systems of the body and keep them functioning optimally. However, these energy meridians are subject to blockage from various causes or in various circumstances. When the meridians become blocked, first symptoms and then illness ensue. If these blockages become constant, the person goes into allergic stress and chronic and degenerative illnesses develop.

Everything - people, animals, plants, foods, chemicals, earth, metals, crystals, etc. - has its own specific energy frequency. Some of these energies can, like the tone of a tuning fork, be very pure. A crystal would have a pure frequency. Other frequencies would be like a complex chord played by an entire orchestra, separate instruments playing together, full of different notes, overtones, and complexities. An animal or a complex substance like a chocolate chip cookie would be a complex and not necessarily harmonious chord.

Inevitably, some of these energies are incompatible with the energy of the human body. For instance, the energy of potassium cyanide is incompatible with everyone's energy, and kills everybody. However, if someone has allergies or an allergic disposition, things with energies that are compatible with non-allergic people are incompatible with them (whether they are born with these incompatibilities, develop them according to a genetically determined schedule, or develop them though exposure). It is as if substances that are benign or even beneficial to non-allergic persons are toxic to them.

What happens when an allergic person is exposed to a substance with an incompatible energy, an allergen? The body marshals its defenses as if to a toxic attack. One of the things that happen when the body marshals its defenses is that one or more meridians close down. This blocks the energy to the organs which this meridian serves, and starts a symptom or disease process, alerting you to the danger at hand.

Although she never stated it as such, my psychologist's mind quickly picked it up; Dr. Nambudripad's theory of what happens when an allergen is treated by NAET boils down to physical "deconditioning or unlearning". If the body can experience an allergen without the meridian closing down, it can unlearn its reactivity, and relax into compatibility. Through the treatment process, the meridians get unblocked while in the presence of the allergen that caused them to block in the first place. This allows the body to "unlearn" its reaction to the substance; so the allergy ceases; so the theory goes.

The "magic secret" of auto-kinesiology or finger-testing

Without a complete understanding of what we were doing, Jeanie and I went for weekly clearings regularly until Rich announced he was going on a three-week vacation. I took the occasion to ask him to explain to Jeanie and me the rudiments of testing and clearing, so that if something came up we could handle it ourselves. He agreed and showed us how to do a generic clearing that would work most of the time.

But more importantly, he revealed to us the secret of his magical powers. It had always mystified me how, just by touching people, he could tell if they were allergic to something, as well as whether they were now clear, how long they had to avoid the allergen and so on, all crucial parts of the NAET process.

It turned out that the "trick" that gave him his magical powers was a variant of kinesiology or muscle testing. What he did was use his index finger in lieu of the testee's arm and try to press it down with his middle finger. If his finger was weak and gave way, it was an indication of an allergy, a weakness, a positive, or a "yes" answer. If it

23

held strong, there was no allergy or weakness, or it was a "no" answer. Just like testing an arm, except for one thing, he wasn't testing our arms; he was testing his own fingers and getting the same answers! The official explanation of the way kinesiology worked was that the allergy blocked an energy meridian, thus weakening the muscles. (How could this explain his being able to test our arms on his fingers?)

The finger technique doubtless evolved something like this. First, kinesiologists discovered that when on occasion you cannot test another person's arm, say they are too sick or young or otherwise unable to cooperate, you can use a surrogate. The surrogate has only to touch the patient, and you can test him just as you can test the patient. Evidently through touch, the energy, whatever that is, flows through to the surrogate and weakens his arm in the same way as the patient. Finger testing is a means of self-testing. However, it stands to reason that, if you can use other people as surrogates, you can use yourself as a surrogate as well, by the simple expedient of touching the patient and testing yourself. So far so good.

Some practitioners, however, independently came to the discovery that you can also test patients without touching them or even being in their vicinity. As the distance between doctor and patient increases, the energy flow between them of necessity decreases and with it the plausibility of the meridian explanation. My experiences with Rich, and then my work and Jeanie's, led me to accept the validity of the testing (at least most of the time), but not the validity of the explanation. Something far weirder was afoot. Kinesiology, the esoteric arm of chiropractic, had entered the twilight zone and me with it! My world view, up to now dependent on either denying paranormal phenomena (which clearly this was) or explaining it away, was being stretched to its breaking point. I used to dismiss paranormal reports by saying when I experienced them first hand; I'll try to account for them. Well, now I had, and I couldn't.

I had to find an explanation, and I realized that like the simultaneity question of Einstein, this kinesiological parlor trick was threatening the boundaries of my universe. If my universe shattered, it would have to be put back together in an altogether different shape. Even more seriously, I realized I was missing at least one essential piece that, like Einstein's concept of relativity, had to be found before my universe could come together again in any shape whatsoever.

When Rich showed us how to do clearings and then left us to our own devices, it sparked an explosion of involvement and exploration in us that was so intense it continues unabated until this day, so much so that I count it as another beginning to this story. We must have been destined to do this work because as soon as we learned the basic technique, we started not only clearing ourselves on anything and everything, but also questioning and exploring the techniques and their implications. And as we did, our sense of what was possible began to expand in unforeseen directions.

Chapter 2
Self-Empowerment in an Age of Experts

In the past half-century quantum physics has been learning what the spiritual traditions of the world have been telling us for millennia, namely, that there is another level of connection by which "things" communicate, interact, and influence one another. In physics this is called the quantum field; in biology it is being called the morphogenic field (see the work of Rupert Sheldrake). Now, philosopher of science Ervin Laszlo postulates that there is an Akashic field or an A field in which all information, throughout time, is recorded, and from which it can be retrieved. Because I am writing about a particular amalgam of psychology and consciousness, I am calling it the psychonoetic field and calling the connection to it, the psychonoetic connection. (However, I want to emphasize that the "psychonoetic field" is just another way, a "scientific" way of referring to what I described as universal or God consciousness in the previous chapter.)

On the material plane, we are used to things communicating, interacting and influencing one another through the process of cause and effect described by Newtonian or classical physics. But when "things" interact on the quantum or psychonoetic plane, they do so in ways that flout the laws of classical physics. Rather than taking time, interactions are instantaneous; rather than requiring physical proximity, they are non-local. Rather than being sequential and relying on cause and effect, they are synchronous; and rather than being factual and objective, they are dependent on the act of observation or perception. (The "laws" of quantum physics bear more than a coincidental similarity to the way consciousness works.)

Furthermore, although not everyone would agree with this by a long shot, interactions in the psychonoetic field seem responsive to conscious intention. In some profound sense things in this realm do not have a material existence; rather they are creations of the beholder, created by the act of perception.

Learning to operate in the psychonoetic realm connects us to an authoritative source of inner knowledge, which in turn frees us from dependence on other authorities, be they doctors, therapists or spiritual teachers. As the connection deepens, new frontiers of self-knowledge and self-direction start to open up. Not only can you find out the answers to almost anything you want to know about yourself...all sorts of things about your body, your mind, your emotions...but you can also decide to let go of irrelevant or mistaken information, to adjust some aspect of your consciousness to better fit your present reality, or even modify your body's functioning to better accommodate present circumstances.

There are many channels of communication within our bodies and minds, sensory, chemical, neural, etc., and many of these can also be said to give us self-knowledge and self-direction. However, overarching all of these is the much more comprehensive psychonoetic connectedness of every part of us to every other part. The psychonoetic connection allows us to communicate and transform ourselves with pure intention, to be psychic within our own bodies and minds. Most of us are unaware that this psychonoetic dimension of connectedness exists and that it is a priceless tool to be used in transforming our lives. But exist it does, and this book starts you using it.

The age of experts

We live in the ultimate age of specialization. Never before in history has life been subdivided into so many separate compartments requiring separate experts for each compartment. Vast sectors of our world have become too complicated for the normal person to function in. Everywhere we look there are specialties within specialties. Scientists specialize in one branch of knowledge, physicians specialize in one disease, executives specialize in one job, and automobile mechanics specialize in one part or one make of car. And we all experience this compartmentalization, this separation, in our daily lives as everything we do becomes more isolated from everything else.

In addition, we are separated laterally by nationality, race, education and income, and separated generationally by a technology gap. Every new generation takes for granted the technological environment in which it grows up, is but the same technology is a challenge for the next, older generation and sometimes insurmountable for the generation older than that. Baby boomers struggle with their computers while their parents mostly stand in mystified awe of them. But for our young, computers are toys.

Even self-care has become professionalized

Nothing in this maze of compartmentalization has become more specialized than the way we care for ourselves. Everything from birth to death has moved into the hands of experts and their facilities. We give birth hooked up to machines and die the same way. We treat birth as if it was a medical emergency, and extreme age as if recovery was possible. Sick or well, we live under the care of medical doctors. A similar situation prevails in education and even our emotional and spiritual lives. We are educated not in the home, community, or workplace, but in schools by professional teachers. The remainder of our private lives are carved up and shared out among an army of social workers, counselors, psychologists, nutritionists, physical fitness coaches, rabbis, and priests. We even play under supervision. We are told what to eat, how to dress, how to talk, walk, exercise and above all, what to buy - by experts in their fields. Moreover, every expert is, of necessity, a salesman, and the common denominator of every almost every sale is *giving over your authority.*

Perception and specialization

What is not widely appreciated is that this separation and compartmentalization comes from the way perception works. In order for the mind to think, it has to first label and separate things into words or ideas so that they can be manipulated like objects. The rampant specialization that has come over just about every imaginable field of human endeavor is not an evil plot so much as it is a side effect of our perceptual processes which name and categorize everything and everyone.

Testing has mesmerized us

Part of the way specialists establish their authority over our own knowing is to find ways to test us. Physicians, teachers, psychologists, counselors, coaches, and nutritionists: all test and measure before they advise, prescribe, and treat. High tech, high cost testing has become part of life and the major part of modern medicine. The machines have mesmerized us. The higher the technology, the more we believe in the instruments; and the more we believe in the instruments, the less we believe in ourselves. Yet, tests are simply procedures for observation and measurement, and the complicated gadgets specialists use to test us are simply extensions of our senses. Just because a machine does the testing and analyzing, does not mean it is better or even as good as informed observation, or even expert introspection.

We have accepted that we do not know how to care for ourselves...In fact, we have accepted that, in general, we do not know!

Individually and as a society, we have become convinced that we need these specialists to care for ourselves. We have accepted that by and large we do not know how to care for ourselves, or at the very least, that the experts know better. In some cases we simply have been sold a bill of goods, while in others the experts really do know better, but only because we have lost touch with ourselves. Of course, there are times when it is wise to consult specialists, but we need to strike a balance and right now we are strongly overbalanced towards dependency.

Admittedly, some of what we get with all this expert care is superior to what we can do for ourselves, and, of course, modern technology offers some real advantages, particularly in medicine. All of it, however, comes at a great expense, not only for us personally, but for society as a whole.

When self-care becomes professionalized, it becomes an economic commodity. Health care and education cut two of the biggest slices out of our national budget, and unnecessarily so. Imagine what the money spent on high tech health care and pharmaceuticals could contribute to the financial well-being of us all.

However, the greatest cost is not in money, but in the quality of our lives. Everything that we do not discover and do for ourselves, or through our family or community, makes our lives narrower and less alive. It gets us out of touch with our bodies, our emotions, our real needs and the people around us. Over-dependence also makes us fearful. We know that we are reliant upon a system that doesn't care about us, whose only motivation for supporting us is monetary, maximizing profits while minimizing exposure and accountability.

Submerged in this system, we get further and further from an intuitive knowing of what is best for us - the best care - the best food - the best life. Without some source of real knowledge, no matter how much money we have, we can only be assured that we are getting the most expensive help, without any assurance that it is in any way the best help. Over-reliance on experts invites not simply specialization, but also insecurity, servitude, alienation, and exploitation.

People everywhere are reclaiming their right to self-care

One of the reasons why we rely on experts so much is because we have gotten out of touch with ourselves. On the other hand, we have gotten out of touch by relying on experts. It is a vicious circle, and all of us have to break out of it for ourselves. Fortunately, there is a strong counter movement in our society, a thrust towards simplicity, self-reliance and sustainability, a *taking our life back*, which is cropping up in every area of modern society.

This is nowhere more prevalent than in the area of self-care. We are home schooling or banding together to form alternate schools. We are leaving or renovating the old religions with their rigid, authoritarian principles and forming new ones that integrate the ancient wisdom of the East and tribal cultures. We are studying the meditative disciplines, becoming not only students, but even masters of Zen, Tai Chi Chuan, Yoga and countless others. We are seeking alternate means to mental and emotional well-being, like hypnotherapy, co-counseling and dozens of small new designer therapies, many with spiritual overtones that invite self-responsibility.

We are also disregarding the advice and authority of medical doctors, who, while retaining their monopoly in the sickness business have, in some people's eyes, discredited themselves as experts in the area of wellness. This is evidenced by the way modern medicine has consistently brought up the rear in the fields of nutrition, exercise, stress and relaxation, meditation, environmental pollution, prayer and faith, and every other natural and affordable aid to a healthy life. Increasingly, people are choosing to go to physicians as a last resort, and instead are finding their way through a maze of alternate practitioners, including chiropractors, acupuncturists, homoeopathists, naturopaths, herbalists, nutritionists, and healers. Most of all, however, we are taking care of our own physical health, eating right, exercising, finding out about and taking vitamins and other food supplements, and saying no to pharmaceuticals except as last resorts.

PsychoNoetics offers the power of auto-kinesiological testing and clearing to self-empowerment

At its core, PsychoNoetics is all about empowerment. Through self-testing and clearing, it offers a free, viable and comparably reliable alternative to consultation, prescription and treatment by professionals. PsychoNoetics works on all levels of being, from the physical level where we identify and clear allergies, to the psychological level where we identify and clear memories and mistaken conclusions, to the spiritual level, where we identify and clear false identities so that we can more easily find our real one. With its emphasis on continually returning to the reality of our true nature, the clearing path of PsychoNoetics can reinstate our spiritual core and restore true meaning to our lives.

Discovering PsychoNoetics, the story
Part 3. Exploring the Psychonoetic Realm

You Can Test Any Question on your Fingers

Jeanie mastered finger testing immediately, while I struggled for months before it finally started working. I became so discouraged that I developed a spiritual inferiority complex. I came to feel better about it later when Devi told us that it had taken her two years to master the art.

One of the first discoveries we made about finger testing was that it was not limited to allergies or health questions; you could test a wide variety of yes- or-no questions and get an answer.

It was incredible. As is my tendency, I started to speculate on what it all really meant. At first, we thought it must be limited to what the tester knows on the subconscious level, sort of like hypnosis, and that when you were testing someone, you were tapping into his subconscious. But as we got bolder, we started asking questions that neither of us could know, and we still got answers! Of course, it was hard, sometimes impossible, to validate all of these answers, but answers we got, lots of them! We asked about reincarnation, the meaning of life, what caused a particular illness and what to do in a particular situation. I can't remember what questions I thought up to ask, but I kept them coming all day.

Imagine if you could ask anything you wanted to, and you would get an answer from some unknown oracle. As long as it could be answered yes or no, Jeanie's fingers could answer it. Investigating an issue was like a meaningful game of Twenty Questions, and Twenty Questions has always been a game I liked. Finger testing turned out to be a cornerstone of psychonoetic practice.

In addition to asking questions, we took to treating and clearing one another and Ariel constantly. Our day was taken up with testing and clearing; in three weeks we did more clearing than in the previous ten months. It became an obsession.

And as we tested and cleared, we were getting results. For example, we would feel better immediately after diagnosing and treating a food allergy, or a sneezing fit would end when we discovered the source and cleared it. Success validated us and energized our explorations.

One day I got a bright idea. Part of the NAET clearing procedure was tapping and massaging certain acupressure points (pressure on certain points in the meridian system seems to keep the energy flowing). Does another person have to massage your acupressure points to clear an allergen, I asked myself? What if you could direct your attention and energy to the necessary acu-points while holding the allergen, and clear yourself. Since I had a background in Tai Chi Chuan, an internal martial art out of the same Taoist tradition that developed acupuncture, I was familiar with the concept and the practice of directing energy. In one sense this idea was a natural one for me. Anyway, I tried it, and it worked. Within days of this discovery we were routinely clearing ourselves mentally, and only asking for one another's help when the allergy was wiping us out to the point where we couldn't concentrate, or we were very sleepy. This was an enormous breakthrough because it meant that the word or the thought could substitute for the physical doing, and therefore, that we could clear our own allergies! And if we could do it, others could too!

We clear one another

We made one more discovery in those weeks, and this was to me the most mind-boggling of all. We found that we could do clearings mentally, or if you like – psychically, not only on ourselves, but also on each other!

Jeanie must have dreamed up the technique for Ariel, because at that time, the possibility of psychic phenomena was as unacceptable to my scientific bias as time travel. Ariel (who was 7 at the time), though she was interested and excited at being cleared and clearing herself the first few times she did it, soon found the entire process too boring for words. Not even the promise of an ice cream cone could entice her to do the clearing one more time.

Ariel reminded me of the story the gestalt psychologist Wolfgang Kohler told about Sultan the chimp. Kohler taught Sultan to police his cage. The first few times he did it with enthusiasm, proudly earning the banana that was his reward. But as it got to be old hat, he performed more and more reluctantly, until finally he sat sullenly in the middle of the dirty cage and refused to pick up one apple core even if offered an entire fruit salad for a reward. Sultan had a low threshold for boredom.

Although Ariel shared Sultan's low threshold for boredom, she, unlike Sultan was an allergic child, and it just didn't make any sense to keep her suffering when relief was at hand. So Jeanie, who despite being a physical anthropologist with a heavy research background, was looser and less linear than I, tried various, mental, psychic, or to use the politically correct term, distant healing techniques on her. They seemed to work, although it took a long time for me to come to believe it.

Fundamentally, what Jeanie did was to ask herself whether Ariel was allergic to something, for example, a pollen, and then finger test. If she got a positive answer, she would then repeat something mentally like "clearing Ariel on pollen", while imagining she was stimulating her acupressure points. Then she would test again, and if the test was positive proceed to cross crawl (a process we co-opted from my training in Edu-K, that balances the hemispheres of the brain, and seemed to facilitate our clearings) with the stated intention that it was for Ariel. As I said the technique seemed to work, but I refused to take it seriously…yet.

My personal conversion to space cadet status, however, came scant weeks later. Jeanie got a violent sneezing attack while driving with me on a six-lane freeway. There was no exit in sight. The sneezing attack was disrupting her driving, scaring me so much that my life was flashing before my eyes. Between the sneezing and the traffic, treating herself was out of the question. It was up to me. OK, this is it.

I ran through the mental routine of clearing Jeanie and just for fun I added an extra fillip of my own. To the command to clear on the pollen, I added the command that she immediately stop sneezing. Remember I am mumbling to myself with my eyes closed and testing on my fingers while Jeanie is navigating an unfamiliar five lane interchange in South Seattle, map on the steering wheel and desperately looking for an exit - in the middle of a sneezing attack so violent I was afraid her eyeballs were going to pop out. Not exactly ideal conditions for psychic healing, yet the exact instant, swear to God, that I instructed the inside of my head to please stop Jeanie's sneezing, it stopped!

Pride, disbelief, even fear surged through me. This stuff works. Am I a psychic healer? What is going on? But even then, accompanying all the intense emotions was an acceptance, a sense of the ordinariness of what had just happened. Both of those clusters of feeling have stayed with me. On the one hand, wonder, awe, pride, disbelief, and on the other, a sense of ordinariness, of ordinary miracles. Distant healing is an extension of self-empowerment.

You can transfer treatments

The next technique that we discovered, though even more a stretch, was basically a variation on the last one. Briefly, it consists of transferring an allergy treatment that you already have to somebody else. At the time we discovered we could do it, it didn't seem to be very useful. It seemed just as easy to do an original clearing as to transfer one. But later on, when we were attempting much more ambitious psychic healing stunts, it became invaluable.

For instance, if Jeanie or I came down with a virus, we would try to psychically transfer the information to the immune systems of everyone else in the household, so they could start manufacturing antibodies before becoming infected and thus avoid getting sick. It was psychic vaccination. Again, it's hard to prove that this was really working, but our fingers said it was, and there seemed to be a lot more instances where one person would catch a cold or flu and no one else would get it. Transferring treatments or immunities is both an extraordinary possibility and a primary psychonoetic tool!

I adjust Jeanie's thyroid

An even more dramatic discovery came about one night, almost by accident, a couple of months later. It was after midnight, and I was watching a late movie in the bedroom while Jeanie slept. Now, Jeanie is usually cold and sleeps bundled up under heavy covers, while I am just the opposite. This evening I looked over, saw the huge bump which I assumed somewhere at its center, must hold Jeanie (sleeping under all the quilts we owned), and I got an idea.

I asked my fingers for a one to ten rating on Jeanie's thyroid function. I got a three, which I thought was pretty low. So without waking her, I asked my fingers if Jeanie's thyroid function could be reset to a ten, and then I did it. Then, I forgot all about it and got into my movie. After about forty-five minutes, however, Jeanie became restless, and I watched fascinated while still sleeping, she kicked off the blankets, one by one until she was sleeping completely uncovered, except for her flannel nightgown and white socks (a sexier sight, man has never known). So now I had something new in my bag of tricks, reading and resetting all sorts of glandular and organ functions.[2]

The psychonoetic connection

It was at this point that we began to reify what was happening...we started referring to the "psychonoetic field". It became our language for noting that by going within our own psyches, we could access immense amounts of information as well as impact our friends and family! We came to understand the language of the religious traditions when they speak about finding the kingdom of God within, or about focusing on a point within to open the doorway to the universe. What we were experiencing seemed to be only the beginning.

To be continued...

---

[2] Jeanie and I have had major discussions on the ethics of psychically influencing another person this way. We note that we live in a world where institutional interests, i.e., governments, schools, organized religions, special-interest groups, various health and medical establishments, and, of course, every company that is trying to sell us stuff **is trying to impact our psyche all the time!** What is more, for the most part, they do it not out of concern for our benefit, but for their own! It seems to me that systematically avoiding all psychic influence over people, no matter what the benefit to them, in a world where influencing others for one's own benefit is ubiquitous, is not only over scrupulous but constitutes leaving the field to those who have no ethical compunctions whatsoever. The intention is much more important than the action. If one's intention is purely for the highest good, that is the important thing. We need more proactive influences on the side of integrity and truth, to counteract those who would use us.

However, there is a safeguard built into PsychoNoetics which, as I have come to understand it now, is about clearing mistaken conclusions of the mind and the body. If we confine our work to that, to clearing away the untrue and letting the true emerge spontaneously, I think we can do no wrong. We're doing God's work. In this spirit I sometimes clear all humanity, and do it with a joyous heart and a sense of rightness. I do not see it as manipulating, but rather as healing.

Chapter 3
The Psychonoetic Field

All our parts are integrated in the psychonoetic field

There are numerous physiological, chemical, and neurological mechanisms by which the parts of our body/mind communicate with one another and synchronize their efforts. Overarching all these mechanisms is the psychonoetic field that integrates all our parts into one, and connects us to the all mankind. Because all parts of all beings are connected through the psychonoetic field, anyone can potentially connect with any part of himself or anyone else through this field.

Most people are only familiar with psychic or extrasensory powers as the miraculous means by which some gifted individuals read and sometimes heal other individuals. Far fewer people recognize the existence of the quantum or psychonoetic field and realize that it is by tapping into this field that psychics work. When we learn to work in this field, we develop the ability to read and adjust the component parts of ourselves in a way that defies ordinary reality. The corollary to this, which is also not commonly realized, is that in order to really know, communicate with, and heal ourselves, we have to use the psychonoetic field.

We have let our psychic abilities atrophy

Of course, I know that there is a wide spectrum of belief about the very existence of psychic powers and the psychonoetic dimension, ranging from total skepticism to unquestioning faith in television psychics. Speaking as a trained scientist that has come from total skepticism to cautious belief through personal experience, I can certainly sympathize with this. I myself have moved beyond an initial astonishment that psychic phenomena exist, into trying to explore them "scientifically", use them systematically, and accommodate them into a wider world view, not as "unexplainable" miracles, but as *undeniable aspects of being that have explanatory value in themselves*.

It is true that western science, indeed Western culture as a whole, does not readily recognize a psychic dimension. There are several reasons for this. First of all, we are very outwardly directed, relying almost exclusively on language for communication, and the senses and their technical extensions for observation. Psychic phenomena rely on a capacity that is outside of perception, and therefore outside of ordinary knowing or perceptual experience.

Secondly, psychic phenomena do not obey the same rules as ordinary phenomena. In fact, they take place in the same realm of reality as quantum physics. Causality, distance, time, space, etc. do not exist in the same way in the psychic or subtle energy worlds as in the "material"worlds. Indeed, psychic phenomena neither exist on a par with ordinary perceptual phenomena nor behave on a par with them. Instead, psychic phenomena seem to obey completely different rules and even to have some sort of intrinsic intelligence or will of their own. This makes it difficult to contain and demonstrate them with controlled experiments, and even more difficult to replicate these experiments.

Even a generation or so ago this claim would have seemed suspect or even preposterous. However, the last forty or so years have seen the ascendancy of quantum physics, that branch of physics which goes beneath the commonsensical observed universe toward the counterintuitive, the underlying, unknowable reality and has found time and time again that the quantum level does not obey the same rules as ordinary phenomena. The frontiers of physics are documenting a fundamental reality which, at the very least, does not counter-indicate psychic phenomena.

Even the hoary argument of enthusiasts that only true believers can see psychic phenomena, gains credibility in light of quantum physics. One of the cornerstones of the new physics is Heisenberg's uncertainty principle, which states that you cannot observe a phenomenon without affecting it. Another way of saying this is that the beliefs of the observer do indeed affect the observation of psychic occurrences.

If you listen to the official line of our dominant culture, or if you subscribe to a Newtonian materialism in science, you will probably assume, as I once did, that psychic capacities are imaginary. However, if you observe people who have developed psychic capacities and experience what they can do, or better yet develop your own psychic capacities, you might change your mind.

There is one class of people in our society that make their living using psychic capacities. I am referring to psychic healers. Among them are healers that instinctively "know" where to place their hands, and medical intuitives that work with physicians to diagnose puzzling cases and in some cases devise treatment strategies. There is also a psychic dimension to many modes of alternative medicine that use kinesiological diagnosis (muscle testing) for health problems. And, of course, psychic healers do their work over great distances as easily as if the patient was right before them.

Tribal societies use the psychonoetic field far more than we do

Since Western society actively disbelieves in psychic capacities, they have not been developed, but on the contrary, ignored and allowed to atrophy. However, there are some societies who, as a whole, recognize the psychonoetic dimension, value psychic abilities, and award special priestly or shamanistic status to adepts.

Tribal peoples that make their living as hunter/gatherers live far closer to the psychonoetic dimension and use the psychonoetic connection far more than we do. Sickness is dealt with by a visit from the shaman who intercedes in the spiritual world where the ultimate cause of the problem is frequently thought to reside. Usually, this shaman is also an accomplished herbalist, and even here the spirit world is at work, prescribing the right herbs and leading the shaman to them. This same shaman is also a priest tending to the spiritual well-being of the tribe, interceding with the gods on their behalf, and advising them on the good and bad times for any undertaking from making love to making war.

The psychonoetic dimension is so much a part of the life of some tribes that it is taken for granted. It helps lead people to food, warn them of danger, track animals, and keep them from getting lost in the wild. Anthropologists and hunters who have accompanied tribal people on hunting and gathering expeditions have come back with stories of how seemingly miraculous their skills were.

Most tribal peoples have initiation rituals, many which include fasting and enduring torturous ordeals, in order to develop their psychic abilities. In some tribal cultures only a shaman undergoes these initiations, but in others it is part of becoming an adult. There are even some cultures where anyone can elect to become a shaman. It is recognized as a universal human capacity.

Cultural anthropology, observing from the self-appointed wisdom of "science", tends to view these transformational and shamanistic rituals as tribal superstitions devoid of objective reality. But from another viewpoint, these are valid transformational, psychic and healing experiences which concentrate the mind, strengthen the will, and bring people closer to realizing their psychic and psychonoetic capacities.

Fortunately, it is not necessary to fast for a month, hang from hooks sunk into your flesh, meditate naked in a cave in the dead of winter, or endure any "tribal" initiations to realize your psychonoetic abilities. (It will, however, be helpful to do some breathing and relaxation exercises, clear your mind, center your spirit, be moderate in your habits, practice harmlessness, and concentrate your intention.)

We use the psychonoetic field without realizing it

Often, we use the psychic and psychonoetic capacities in our daily life without realizing it. When we intuitively trust or distrust someone or "see their light", we are often really sensing their energy or unconsciously seeing their aura. This is the psychonoetic communication at work.

There is an oft-quoted study in which children were presented a varied buffet to choose from over a period of weeks. They eventually worked out a perfectly balanced diet. How did they know what their bodies needed? That is the psychonoetic communication at work.

Some people use Ouija boards, swing pendulums, consult the Runes or throw the I Ching for guidance in making life decisions, while a lot of us rely on what we may variously think of as intuition, gut feelings, hunches, or the urging of the heart. Sometimes to do something, eat something, or go someplace just doesn't feel right, while other times we feel impelled in certain directions. Some of these experiences come from the psychonoetic field, but others do not. A lot of our "intuitive" impulses come from being in memory, and are really unconscious, emotional reactions. If we are to safely navigate in psychic seas, we have to refine our navigational tools and skills.

Contamination of the psychonoetic field with emotion, is the most common obstacle to intuitive and psychonoetic communications. Because intuitive channels are so amorphous, it is easy to get true intuition confused with fear on the one hand, and wishful thinking on the other. Yet people who listen to their inner voices function better, enjoy more success, and get into less trouble than people who *only* evaluate things intellectually. How do we avoid throwing out the baby with the bath water. The first thing we can do is cultivate all of our faculties, including intellectual judgment and common sense, and use them in a balanced way. In addition, PsychoNoetics should always be used in partnership with information, reasoning, and when appropriate, professional consultation. Psychonoetic communications should be as carefully evaluated for accuracy as any other information. (You'll learn various methods for doing this in this book. In general however, you'll find that psychonoetic techniques are conservative and include safeguards.)

The psychonoetic field connects us all

In terms of utilizing the psychonoetic field, it seems to make relatively little difference whether the consciousnesses in question are components of one individual, or are associated with separate individuals. They can be accessed similarly. This supports the conclusion that not just individuals, but the totality of mankind are psychically integrated.

This is not mysterious or magical, although it can seem that way. The psychonoetic field is more than an extension of the knowing by which all living things know themselves. It is an aspect of being.

Discovering PsychoNoetics, the story
Part 4. Expanding into Psychology

Clearing core beliefs

By the time Rich got back, we weren't sure we needed him anymore. In fact, I was feeling so full of myself that I thought we had passed him flying. Of course, it wasn't true. Although we had worked out a few techniques he hadn't suspected, he was a proficient NAET practitioner with a lot to teach us. After some procrastination we went back to him, anxious to check on our unconventional clearings among other things. Were our mental and distant clearings really working, or were we delusional? To our satisfaction, Rich confirmed that we were really clear on the things we had cleared ourselves.

At this point we didn't tell Rich much about the way we were doing things. There were two reasons. One, he was a little insecure, I suspect because he only had a massage therapist license then (in the process of becoming an acupuncturist), and most of the people practicing NAET were already chiropractors or acupuncturists; he was careful to do his practice by the book. Two, we suspected we had discovered the Holy Grail, and no one else knew what we knew, so we were guarding it. This turned out only to be partially true. Officially NAET was all meridians and energy, but when we started training and going to symposiums, we found out that quite a few people, including Devi herself, had ventured into the twilight zone of parapsychology. However, no one seemed to be exploring it with quite the same zeal that we were. (Perhaps, like us, they were psychically-challenged!)

During one of our visits, Rich put us on to a very interesting sidelight of the work, one that gave us the first connection between NAET allergy clearings [more or less a physical phenomenon] and the mind. This we soon formulated as core belief revision. This is how it happened.

Jeanie was having trouble retaining a treatment to something or other. Every time Rich cleared her she "blew" the treatment. Finally, he suggested she say the following sentence, "I want to be sick." He finger-tested on this just as he would finger-test on an allergen, and lo and behold the finger went down, a "yes" answer. Next, he had her repeat the sentence while he went through her back's acupressure points, and then repeat, "I don't want to be sick," while he did points on her hands and feet. Then, he had her repeat, "I want to be sick" and tested her again. This time the test was negative. Treating her meridians on a belief had cleared it and reversed it.

Then Rich repeated the original clearing, I don't remember what it was on, and this time it held. Discovery: you can clear a negative belief just as you can a negative substance or allergen.

Once again the plot thickens! Core belief revision is another possibility through the "psychonoetic connection"! Another discovery: allergy and belief or body and mind are interdependent, and this interdependence is important to self-healing and self-empowerment.

Jeanie was very impressed when Rich did this core belief clearing. For some reason it went right by me, although I know I was there at the time. Perhaps, it was because having endured eight hard and expensive years of training as a psychologist and psychoanalyst, I tend not be too impressed (either that or too territorial), when a massage therapist or chiropractor has you repeat something a few time, thumps on your back and pronounces you cured of a psychological problem. However, although I still think (or hope) that the mind is vastly more complicated than chiropractic gives it credit for being, Rich certainly was on to something!

Anyway, Jeanie realized right away that mind-body interdependence went beyond the limited application of freeing up resistant allergies. She intuited that core beliefs were critical in forming and sustaining allergies and that whenever allergies were cleared, core beliefs needed to be explored, identified, and cleared. So the ensuing weeks were devoted to finding, exploring, and clearing negative beliefs about ourselves (including beliefs unrelated to allergies or other health issues).

The training

By the time we had developed all this stuff, I thought we were ready to go into business ourselves. So we decided to take the NAET training. Actually, I had been talking about taking the training for some time. For months, every time I gave Rich a check for a hundred bucks, I thought it would not only be easier, but much cheaper to learn the complete "how to" ourselves.

Since the time when Rich went on vacation, however, I discovered a vocation. It was as if I had been born to do NAET, or more precisely, to do something of which NAET was a starting point. Jeanie, as usual, was more ambivalent, but between her bouts of ambivalence she was as much into it as I was, and contributing new ideas constantly. Someone who believed in the Jungian idea of synchronicity might say that the universe gave me allergies to prime me for the revolution in consciousness that was taking place in me, as I sat with the "paranormal" implications of our discoveries.

What revolution in consciousness you may ask; I haven't heard anything about a revolution in consciousness. Just wait; it's coming.

For now there's only a loosening of the soil, a thorough roto-tilling of the hard packed clay of my preconceptions, as I experienced my first "psychic"or at least unexplained phenomenon, not in the form of second or third party reports that I could dismiss, but as my own, undeniable experiences. Can one find God in allergy clearing? Well, easier than in a bottle of antihistamines!

Just what are we doing?

We now had to find some way to build a bridge from our backgrounds in psychology and anthropology to NAET. Actually, we were worrying about this problem long before we took the training, but when we were ready to start treating people the problem became acute. For me, the body-mind connection was in core belief revision. If NAET could be fruitfully placed in a context with other, more psychological factors, at least my background could stretch to cover it. What if we did not do NAET, but something broader which included NAET? It could cover not only NAET, but also core belief revision, psychotherapy, hypnotherapy, education, and support. Not only might it better rationalize our backgrounds, but it might be better allergy therapy as well. After all, didn't all of these factors come into allergies, and were not most of the problems with clearing and holding treatments in NAET due to emotional factors or belief systems?

Besides, what really was happening in an NAET treatment? Devi explained it as an energy phenomenon related to Chinese medicine, but was that the whole truth? Of course, there was something happening on an energy level in allergy, just as there was something happening on a physical level, for example, sneezing, but was that the central or most relevant level? If NAET worked only with the acupressure protocol, I might have bought this explanation, but it worked verbally and psychically as well, which ruled out meridian energy as the primary explanation for me.

Chinese medicine seemed to me to waffle on the nature of chi or energy. When they struggled to be accepted as an insurable health care modality, on a par with chiropractic, conventional medicine, and dentistry, acupuncturists were very adamant about the physical reality of chi, i.e., that it is a real energy obeying physical Newtonian laws and circulating in real channels. However, the history of Chinese medicine is unlike physical medicine as we know it, and the original descriptions of chi and meridians were as subtle or psychic energy. This is a very important distinction, because if chi is physical energy, the meridian model fails to explain NAET's ability to work through the psychic dimension. If chi is subtle or psychic energy, this is less of a problem.

Before I go on, I have to explain something unusual about the relationship between Jeanie and I. We are both scientists intensely interested in both theory and spirituality. We spend many happy hours in bed arguing about topics like evolution and enlightenment. In Miami I had started a book on the way perception constructs reality (since published by Paragon House under the title of <u>Oneness Perceived, A Window Into Enlightenment),</u> and had honed many of its concepts with Jeanie. Now we set ourselves to the task of figuring out just what was happening with NAET.

The first thing we agreed on was that allergies and their reversal didn't just involve the energy body, whatever that is, or the physical body for that matter. Allergies involved the whole person on as many levels as existed. The other thing we decided was that perception was a likely candidate for the central mover in the whole phenomenon of allergy.

Making it as simple as possible, something, some consciousness, on some level, comes to perceive a relatively innocuous substance as toxic, i.e., an allergen, and something in the NAET treatment or other related treatment reverses that perception. Moreover, the perception of an innocuous substance as an allergen is related to the person's physical state, belief systems, emotions, memories, and Lord knows what else. Based on this analysis, we came up with the following position paper.

Allergy Healing Modalities

NAET views allergy principally as a response of the body or energy body to an allergen, something which for some reason has come to be mistaken as a threat to its survival. The allergen is the cause; the allergic symptoms are the effect. This is an accurate, but partial picture.

The expanded view we came to is that an allergy is a perceptual mistake in which the allergic symptom is only one manifestation of a whole constellation of ensuing disturbances which exist simultaneous on a body, mind, emotional, and energetic level. Often the allergic symptom is not even the most debilitating disturbance, just the one which is most evident and most difficult to ignore. Following this shift in paradigm we started treating the whole "perceptual" constellation, not just the allergy. Not only did we get better, more permanent results this way, but we started getting "peripheral" benefits which in some cases were even more beneficial than clearing the physical allergy. People started getting relief from problems which they didn't know were related to the "allergy", problems which were emotional, social, and even spiritual. Ultimately, we realized that the allergic symptom, like any other symptom, was telling us that something was amiss with the whole person. We continued to make treating the allergy our first priority, but that led us into treating the whole person. In particular, it led us into finding and correcting the perceptual mistakes that underlay the entire "allergic" syndrome!

What all allergies seem to have in common with one another is that the body/mind recognizes some environmental factor as a threat to its survival. Then, it seems to have two complementary reactions to it. First, it tries to expel it, (sneezing, diarrhea, etc.), but eventually it becomes overwhelmed. Over time the expulsion mechanisms tend to become weaker and the chronic degenerative aspects of the allergy predominate.

Allergy Healing Modalities is a holistic and multimodal treatment strategy. It works with the physical, mental, emotional, and energy bodies as is appropriate. Kinesiology is used to locate allergies, and acupressure points are used to re-educate the body/mind that these environmental factors and foods do not pose a threat and therefore do not need to be reacted to.

Next, psychological and emotional factors are addressed. Negative beliefs about self and world predispose people to keep forming allergies and in certain instances undo treatments. These beliefs are identified and revised as part of the AHM strategy. In some instances, moods, emotional upset, trauma, and illness can be responsible for undoing treatments and allergies have to be treated in combination with these. Often different subpersonalities have different allergic profiles, and one has to make sure to diagnose and treat all the major subpersonalities.

AHM is completely safe, comfortable and non-invasive. It uses no injections, drugs, or rotation diets. Once you are cleared for an allergen you either don't react to it, or only have a very mild reaction. For the most part you will be able to live where you want to live and eat what you want to eat, free of the restrictions that allergies place on your life.

Although we were still focusing on allergies (and even offering our new "expertise" to others), it began to occur to me that I was gradually also restructuring all that I knew about psychology, and even beginning to get a better idea of what we mean by the conscious and unconscious minds. I began to see why even Freud had missed the complexity of what we are dealing with in our mental worlds, and why we are so willing to let someone else tell us what is good for us. It's easier than trying to figure ourselves out!

To be continued...

Chapter 4
Every Part of Ourselves is Conscious

Why are we are so easily convinced that the experts, with their tests and their machines, know what is good for us better than we know ourselves? The answer lies in what we fundamentally believe to be true about ourselves. This belief system is almost universal and largely in error. It has three parts:

1. We believe that we are a complex system made up of body, mind and emotions, of many parts and processes, cells, organs, intricate brain structures, hidden feelings, repressed memories, unconscious motives [all of which can go terribly wrong in mysterious ways]. *This is true.*

2. We believe that these parts of ourselves, in and of themselves, are in themselves devoid of intelligence. They are just parts of our biological and psychological machines. They only live through us. *This is false.*

3. We feel that we either don't have any means of knowing anything about our constituent parts, or, at the best, that these means are crude and inexact. *This is false also.*

This is what almost everybody believes, deep down. The first piece of the answer, that we are made up of many parts, is true, in fact probably true beyond our wildest imagining. However, the rest of the answer, that these parts are devoid of intelligence of their own, and that we only have very crude and inexact means of knowing anything about them, is to the same extent, *false*! No wonder we believe that anybody who has a reliable test, a precise method of peering inside of us, knows what is good for us better than we do ourselves. No wonder we are so willing to give control over our lives to the experts.

Let us examine this belief system more closely.

TRUE: *We are made up of many parts*

We are indeed made up of many parts, on many levels of organization, cell, gland, organ, nervous system, ideation, etc. Biologists are beginning to note how intense networking at all these levels underlies the great cooperative unity that we experience as our self. And we know this mysterious complexity intimately.

FALSE: *Our parts are biological machines, without consciousness.*

The common belief that we are biological machines made up of the mechanical parts is a misconception. Many historians have noted that this concept of our bodies as machines has arisen with the advance of humanity into the mechanized age of science and industry. However, we know from experience that each cell in our body vibrates with life and is not a cog in a machine. Think of the rapid healing that is marshaled by the appropriate cells when we cut ourselves.

It is much more consistent with our experience to see that each part of us has its own consciousness and is subject to its own limitations. Each part can be seen, in a very real sense, to be a self, perceiving and responding. Yet, all of these consciousnesses within us are unconscious to our conscious mind. All of these consciousnesses are even unconscious to one another.

[The unconscious, contrary to popular conceptions, isn't one thing or in one place, rather it is embedded in the relation of one part to another throughout our body/mind. Every perceiving center in the physiological body appears conscious to itself, but is not aware of the experience of everything that it perceives, which therefore remains unconscious to it.]

The mind is no more monolithic than the body; it, too, is a composite, a symbiotic, hierarchical organism of separate consciousnesses. Our personalities are divided into parts called sub-personalities or personas, which are unaware or unconscious of one another since their experiences are not shared.

All of these parts of ourselves possess an intelligence of their own. Every cell, neuron, gland, and organ, in every combination, every persona, every identity is a separate body/mind and knows itself as well as we know ourselves. *Just as we know ourselves, what we are feeling, seeing and thinking, the constituent parts of ourselves know themselves,* although what they know might be much more rudimentary than what we ourselves know. Part of this intelligence is some power of perception, some sense of their relevant environment. Thus, a pancreas has a way of getting information about blood sugar levels and regulating insulin in response. And a sub-personality has a way of noting behaviors in others that confirms its biases, and reacting quickly.

We are conscious organisms, both competing and cooperating in a simultaneously competitive and cooperative universe. Furthermore, we are made up of equally conscious organisms (cells, sub-personalities), also competing and cooperating in the universe that is us. The interplay of competition and cooperation is ecology, and when they find a balance, and come to a place of relative stability, that is homeostasis.

In this sense, we are all ecological organisms striving for equilibrium in every respect. We are embedded in an ecological universe that is similarly tending towards equilibrium. This conscious interplay of cooperation and competition between all relevant parts of the system, this ecology tending towards equilibrium is, in the broadest sense, evolution. The temporary resting places of relative stability and balance achieved by a system are all things manifest—species, cells, stars, and us.

Overseeing the hierarchy of consciousness within us

In some sense your body/mind is a hierarchy of consciousnesses with your "I consciousness" at the top. Most, if not all, the consciousnesses in the hierarchy are exclusively concerned with survival, not only their own survival, but the survival of the whole on which their individual survival depends. However, they are not interested in the quality of your life, whether or not you get the girl or get your steak grilled the way you like it. That is for you to worry about. What they learn and what governs their behavior are survival tactics.

These tactics are typically short sighted in relationship to the whole that you experience from your seat at the top of the hierarchy, and you, seeing the whole picture, may wish to change some of these unconscious tactics. For instance, in childhood you may have learned to run like hell when faced with a threatening situation. However, a threatening situation may emerge in later life, like getting a speeding ticket, in which you know it is not in your best interests to run. However, if you cannot release your childhood conditioning, your conscious decision not to run is going to conflict with your preconditioning to run. Conflicts like these make you less able to respond optimally at critical times.

Clearly, if we could communicate directly with our constituent parts, we could avoid internal conflict and learn to cooperate more effectively. The major obstacle to taking this kind of internal authority is our belief that we can't communicate with our parts.

FALSE: We can't communicate with our parts

Most of us believe that we don't have any means of communicating with these parts of ourselves, these unconscious consciousnesses, these silent voices. The truth that most of us do not even suspect is that *there exists a way by which we can communicate with all aspects of ourselves. We can listen to them, talk to them, and in many cases align them to our will!* We communicate with them through the psychonoetic connection. We are, after all, one body/mind.

There are even certain conditions when our unconscious body/minds will bow to our authority. It is as if they know there is something bigger than them, which they are a part of and which they are dependent on. Since they have a hierarchical relationship to us, we have a certain degree of influence over them. Although we do not by any means command total obedience, by building internal relationships of trust, we increase our influence. And if we are successful in establishing trust, we can use our authority to restructure the responses of our unconscious mind in almost any way we choose.

Discovering PsychoNoetics, the story
Part 5. Putting the mind back in

In August we presented our new understandings of consciousness at the NAET annual symposium, and we attended the advanced NAET training seminar. It was as though a pincer of my own thinking and the NAET techniques were bringing me into an enormous shift in my worldview, my personality, and gradually my very life.

We learn to clear emotional blocks

The NAET technique of clearing emotional blockages confirmed everything we had been experiencing. This technique is used to clear an emotional block that is causing an allergy or interfering with the clearing of it. You utilize a protocol of simple questions to find the specific emotional block. The first questions establish what category of life the emotional blockage falls into: love, health, financial, work, or study. Then, a second set of questions zeros in on the problem. The questions are things like, "Do you like yourself?" Third, you ask whether something in the person's life happened to cause the problem. After each of these questions you muscle test, of course, to get a yes-or-no answer.

It is the game of Twenty-Questions again. After you ascertain that something specific has happened, you try to find out what year of the client's life it happened in. Often, as you progress, people will remember specific incidents; however, if they do not, it doesn't seem to make much difference to the final outcome. After the problem is identified, the client holds the thought, and you test his alarm points to see what meridians are blocked. Then, you clear the emotion exactly as you would clear an allergen.

We experimented with this technique and soon discovered that not only does this technique clear the emotional blockages that contribute to allergies, but it can also clear emotional blockages that create personality problems as well. However, it is a cumbersome technique and needs a facilitator or other therapist. We soon learned of a similar, but far easier technique, one that was destined to complete the picture we were forming of the psychonoetic field.

Clearing memories

In the symposium weekend that followed the advanced training, we heard from an unconventional dentist, who was also an NAET practitioner, named Andrew Pallos. He taught us a method of psychological self-help known as the LaChance technique, which is powerful, flexible, and easy to use. However, in order to use it you must have mastered auto-kinesiology, that is, you have to be able to test yourself. You use the LaChance technique when you are feeling emotionally upset. It starts by asking yourself how much in memory you are at the present. You say 10%, test, 20%, test, 30% test, and so on. If you are only 20% in memory, you are to all purposes functioning in the present, the here and now. Any higher, however, and you are in the grip of past memories, and to some extent functioning in the past. When you are feeling emotionally upset and find out you are in memory, you locate the memory. Then, and this is the amazing thing, ônce you locate these memories, you can release them, simply by requesting your subconscious to do so.

We started using this technique in our work and on ourselves, until one day I hit a snag. After blowing up at Jeanie for something inconsequential, I decided to do some memory release work on my explosive temper. However, I couldn't get my memories to clear. On further investigation it turned out that I subconsciously believed that it was necessary to get angry in order to make Jeanie consider what I wanted. Thus, I was subconsciously refusing to release these memories. This presented me with a dilemma and a spiritual choice point. In order to resolve my temper, I first had to give up this form of control over Jeanie. I decided to give up control, but it wasn't so easy. I first had to affirm (which means instructing my subconscious again) that I trusted Jeanie's good will and common sense and that it wasn't necessary to bully her into doing what I wanted. Finally, I worked it out with my subconscious and gave up my temper (in that regard at least). Jeanie has been sweeter and more cooperative ever since.

Discoveries

- *You can't clear what you don't want to clear.*
- *You can clear the reason why you don't want to clear something and then go back to clear memories.*
- *You also have to be willing to clear the underlying reason.*

*After learning the memory clearing technique, I started using it more and more. I still use it to this day, but more rarely, simply because I have cleared out the more obvious memory chains. For about six months I did marathon sessions with myself. Every couple of days, whenever something would upset me in any way, I would check how much I was in memory, and then proceed to **locate, identify, and clear** the memories one by one. Sometimes I cleared twenty or thirty memories around a single emotional reaction. I used to do this in bed, either just before getting up or before going to sleep. I found that as I* *cleared a half dozen or so memories in a single session, I would begin to feel very sleepy until I literally couldn't stay awake any longer.*

Although the sessions were long and tedious, I was very motivated for one very good reason. They worked. The technique was virtually miraculous. I had had these upset reactions to situations all of my life, and then, after a few weeks of memory release sessions, I didn't have them anymore. I was becoming an adult, and everyone was finding me much easier to live with. What's more I was finding it much easier to live with myself. I was calmer, steadier, and more upbeat in every way. I have to tell you I am a psychologist, psychoanalyst, psychosynthesist, hypnotherapist, martial artist, and meditator with a lot of experience both doing therapy on others and being in therapy myself, and I have never found anything like this technique. It was dynamite. It skipped understanding, analysis, regression, abreaction, and sometimes even affirmation, and went straight to release. Memory release work is a mighty weapon in the arsenal of self-empowerment techniques.

I clear Jeanie's memories while she sleeps

Jeanie, however, wasn't so impressed. Memory release was too easy; she still favored gut wrenching revelations and strenuous changes. So one morning in bed I tried an experiment, I tried doing a distant memory release on Jeanie, the same way I would do a distance clearing on an allergy. Jeanie had been relating to me with an undertone of anger for some time. When I talked to her about it, she either denied it or said that there was something there, but she didn't know what it was about.

When I started to distantly read and clear for Jeanie, I got memory after memory when she was 42 years old, so many that I thought something was wrong. Either my testing wasn't working or she wasn't clearing. Finally, I got though the 42's to the 43's, but it took a long time.

When Jeanie woke up, however, I noticed that something had changed in her, that quality of anger seemed gone. I told her what I had done and asked her whether there was something particular that happened when she was forty-two. She said yes, that was when our daughter Ariel was born. Then, a torrent of anger, hurt, and grief about my behavior at that time, came flooding out. Now the point that I am making is not simply that these feelings were there, but that they were there in an unavailable, frozen form that expressed itself as anger. It was an anger that Jeanie wasn't conscious of, so we couldn't defuse it, no matter how hard we tried. This anger had given an ugly undertone to our marriage for six years. Now, however, because of a distant memory release series I had done on Jeanie, one morning lying in bed, without her knowing about it, the feelings were released and available. We talked about them, she cried, I apologized, we cried, and our marriage softened and sweetened.

What is interesting about memory release work is that we don't forget the memories and feelings attached to them when we let go. We remember them! Before being cleared, our memories are enfolded into our perceptions which, of course, makes them invisible. We don't perceive them; we perceive **from** *them. The emotional reactions we have to the* **present***, are based on unconscious emotional preconceptions that we formed in the* **past***. We're functioning in a historical context that we don't even know we have.* **We think we perceive reality, but we're really projecting an interpretation onto reality. We're literally making our own reality through our interpretations of our past experiences.**

To get back to Jeanie, she thought she was mad at me for things I was doing in the ongoing present, things that she interpreted as "just like" things I did when Ariel was born, but it just wasn't so. Not only that, but she was seeing me, all of me, all of the time as that person who disappointed her in those first precious months of motherhood. Releasing these memories enabled her to re-perceive the present - and with it, who I really was.

Discovering PsychoNoetics, the story
Part 6. It comes together in Santa Barbara

Just after the NAET meetings, we moved to Santa Barbara. Santa Barbara, even more than Seattle, if this is possible, was a place where some plant or another was pollinating at all times of the year, and everyone who could, had allergies. We did our usual things to promote ourselves and found very few takers. When we talked about what we did, it seemed that people were either not open or not impressed. The populace seemed to be divided into those who were too closed and those who were too open. The closed ones distrusted alternate medicine entirely and thus us; whereas, the open ones were so far out that we seemed mainstream to them, if not positively old hat. In addition, the place was crawling with alternate practitioners, every one of which claimed to be able to cure allergies as a matter of course. After a while I cooked up the following joke.

Someone asks me, "what you do?" I say, "I bring back people from the dead." They say, "Oh, my homoeopathist does that."

I was proud of this joke and told it to everyone I met, but only rarely did I get a laugh. Finally, I figured out why. They didn't get that it was a joke!

What is the nature of this beast we are riding?

Although business was slow, we were really cooking. In the last year we had made major steps. First, we had been helped with our allergies by a massage therapist practicing a technique loosely based on Chinese medicine. After being convinced through our own experience that the treatment worked, we started asking ourselves why it worked, what could be happening. We tentatively arrived at the following re-formulation.

The unconscious mind, more precisely that part of your unconscious which regulates the immune system, has learned mistakenly that a substance is toxic and is responding to it with a protective and expulsive response. This is the definition of an allergy. An allergic response closes off certain energy pathways or acupuncture meridians in the presence of the allergen. The NAET treatment re-opens these same meridians in the presence of the same allergen and keeps them open, thus reversing the allergic response. The subconscious then experiences the allergen without the allergenic response, sees that nothing bad is happening to the body, and subsequently learns that the substance is not toxic after all. This then "unlearns" the subconscious mistake which caused the allergy!

*It was around this time in what I have come to think of as the great unfolding that we started thinking about the relationship between NAET allergy clearings and the LaChance method of clearing traumatic memories that Andrew Pallos taught us. It became evident to us that they had much in common. After thinking long and hard about it, I came up with the unifying concept of **retroperception.** When you experience something in the present, either emotionally or cognitively or both, as if it is the latest instance of something that has happened in the past, that is a retroperception. Both allergies (physical* *conclusions) and emotional upsets (psychological conclusions) are retroperceptions. All categories of retroperceptions can be cleared intentionally (psychonoetically), changing the reactions of the human psyche, like that of the human immune system, from rejection to acceptance.*

All the different levels of learning and unlearning, physical, emotional, and cognitive, occur in their respective realms, but all of these realms are enfolded in the psychonoetic realm, and regardless of level, they are all retroperceptions. This is why we can identify and clear memories on any level by accessing the psychonoetic realm.

Both allergic and emotional responses are retroperceptions

I saw then that both allergic and emotional responses are retroperceptions, i.e., perceptions made through the lens of past experiences. In the case of an allergy, a substance is perceived as a toxin and exposure to it elicits the same kind of response that the toxin would elicit (the allergic symptom). In a psychological disturbance, a present situation is perceived as being in the same category as a past "traumatic" situation and elicits the same response or symptom, one that, if unjustified, can be inappropriate, counterproductive, and extreme. The situations are highly analogous.

This is a powerful, unifying concept, and I was very excited when it crystallized in my mind. The concept of retroperception allowed me to unite the physiological with the psychological, establishing a body/mind connection. It also provided a common denominator to all sorts of non-pathological psychological difficulties. I could see that, instead of classifying psychological problems separately, psychology could classify most of them as retroperceptions and then go directly to the specific content of each one (which I have largely done in my therapeutic practice).

Retroperceptions

The immune system learns allergies by association. Allergies are learned when formerly innocuous substances are experienced together with other allergic or toxic substances and become associated with them. Allergies, then, are just substances that the immune system has mistakenly learned to consider as toxins. Toxins and allergens alike are lumped together by the unconscious and greeted with the same defensive response. (This suggests that even though allergies can make you sick, allergy formation is an outcome of normal learning and really not a sickness in itself.)

A similar process takes place in the psychological realm, the realm of thoughts and feelings, images, and symbols - all the things memories are made of. Traumatic memories build up defensive categories in the unconscious, like allergic categories form in the immune system. Sickness reactions spawn allergies; traumatic memories spawn defensive categories. When these categories are triggered, the traumatic memories are also triggered, bringing along with them our childhood perceptions, emotions, and reactions, and we get caught in places that we wish to have outgrown.

The way we order our world

Building self-concepts and world-concepts out of memories and then fitting new things into them unconsciously, is the principal way we order our world. It is a process of learning and generalizing that facilitates our recognition of things and events and tells us how to react to them. It is learning and generalizing through association. When appropriate, that is, in areas where there is sufficient continuity for what is learned to remain applicable, it is very efficient. It shortens reaction time and spares our conscious minds for other work. This seamless integration of an already learned, unconscious category with the ongoing stream of conscious experience is fundamental to the process of perception.

However, in discontinuous areas, where the category is no longer valid or the response no longer appropriate, seeing through a past perception is counterproductive. It either misleads us, or at best requires that we consciously oppose our "natural" reactions. Thus, in the same way that allergy formation is an outcome of normal learning and not a physical sickness, perceiving through our past experiences and conclusions is an outcome of normal learning, and not a psychological illness. This, however, does not rule out the possibility that it can make us react in extremely negative and dysfunctional ways, which in turn can make us ill. A retroperception, then, is the unconscious framing of present perceptions in the context of past, formative memories. In other words, when the unconscious identifies something happening in the present with something that happened in the past, that is a retroperception. Even more, when you react to something as if you are the same as you were in the past, often with the emotions of a child, that is definitely a retroperception!

What memories are

I also got a lot clearer about what memories are. A memory is not like a snapshot of something that has happened, but more like a painting, an interpretive and subjective projection. Actually, memories have a dual aspect because in addition to being interpretations of what is happening, they are also conclusions. (More specifically, they are conclusions after the fact and interpretations before the fact.)

What is more, memories are interpretations from the viewpoint of the perceiver. Whatever the bias of the perceiver is, biases the memory. The biased memory, in turn, leads to a conclusion. This conclusion further modifies the viewpoint from which we perceive and builds the context by which we interpret the next "memory" - and the next after that. We see, then, that memories do not exist in isolation, but constitute a cycle of interpretation and conclusion, a progressive viewpoint, an evolving concept of self and world.

Defensive self-concepts are memories built on an event that is experienced as traumatic [usually but not necessarily taking place in childhood]. The perceptions that follow are interpreted as offering further evidence, and widen the application of the original conclusion.

For an example, let's take abandonment. Let us say that a girl has a traumatic memory of being abandoned by her father. Now, it might not be abandonment from the viewpoint of the father. It might be a custody dispute from a divorce, or military service. However, if it is experienced as abandonment, that is all that is important from the point of view of the child. If it is experienced as abandonment, it is remembered as abandonment.

This memory, then, like any interpretation, enters into further perceptions as a preconception. In keeping with this, the girl could conclude either that all men are unreliable, or that she is unworthy, or both. Either way this leads to the conclusion that abandonment is inevitable, which becomes the viewpoint in which additional "abandonments" by friends and lovers are anticipated. Thus, the person builds up a case where, on one hand, they are unworthy, and,

71

on the other hand, the people around them are unreliable. Either way, abandonment is anticipated.

Even after the girl has reached adulthood, she has a tendency to see any distancing behavior as abandonment and react to it with the helpless feelings of an abandoned child. That she is no longer a helpless child is instantly forgotten as she goes into a defensive and panicky overreaction.

To equate trivial distancing with parental abandonment and respond to it with childhood emotions is obviously a perceptual mistake and an extremely undesirable one at that. It leads to the sort of emotional overreactions that clinical psychology portrays as neurotic symptoms. Also, it is structurally very similar to what happens in allergy formation, when you associate a relatively innocuous substance with a toxic one and overreact to it with a defensive response because of an historical context. Both of these perceptual mistakes are retroperceptions, and both may be cleared!

I came to understand that what happens in memory release work is that we disidentify from these memories or self-concepts, thus regaining the ability to experience the present as just what it is, without pre-judgments. We still perceive things from our own viewpoint, but this viewpoint will no longer have concealed within it, a negative self-concept, spawned in a traumatic childhood, and subconsciously brought to the table of the present. The concept of retroperception was the key piece in the puzzle. After I got this piece, the whole picture began to appear.

Beyond allergies to health; beyond retroperceptions to sanity

It is clear what happens when we get beyond the physical retroperceptions that create allergies, we simply become healthier. But what happens when we clear the psychological retroperceptions that cloud our present perceptions? We become saner. We access a level of sanity far beyond our present, subjective distortions, and also, far beyond the consensual reality of our society. We become in touch with an increasingly unbiased reality, a reality seen through an optically perfect lens. I call this seeing of unbiased reality **"radical sanity"**.

Radical sanity is essential to real "spiritual" growth. People for the most part are entrained and entranced by their individual stories. In these stories they portray themselves as less, usually far less than they really are. Building upon a base of childhood perception, most of our stories portray us as more or less helpless, more or less reactive to people and external events, more or less victims, and more or less powerless. All of these are identities that may have passed away with childhood or may never have been a reality, but are now impeding our growth and development. As those stories fall away, with the clearing of memory/conclusions, our real identity, our real power, starts spontaneously manifesting itself.

Chapter 5
In Memory

And there I leave my story for now. So much has continued to unfold in my awareness, but I have shared that first cracking of my old paradigm as it has led me inexorably toward the self-transformational discipline I now call PsychoNoetics. (The word is an amalgam of psychology, the science of mind, and noetics, the science of consciousness.) This crystallization of PsychoNoetics comes from all that I learned from NAET, my explorations with Jeanie, all of my psychological training and spiritual background, and in some sense from all of my life's experiences. It is a deep inquiry into consciousness and the mind, with simple applications for health, well-being, and spiritual growth.

The essence of PsychoNoetics is freeing the body/mind of its contractions and delusions by clearing memories. Yet, what we mean by a memory is not always clear. A memory is commonly looked at as a snapshot of past, stored in the mind like some kind of digital slide. In a lot of psychotherapeutic systems, not only is a memory a snapshot of the past, but it is also a repository of negative, traumatic energy.

However, what I now understand is that memories are also conclusions, conclusions that we have arrived at through interpreting what is happening to us. But even that understanding does not go far enough. What it does not take into account is that the way in which we interpret what is happening to us, is in itself conditioned by prior conclusions.

Let us take a hypothetical example. One child hits a second child at the schoolyard. Now an "objective observer" can attach all sorts of interpretations to this act. One set of interpretations presumes that the second child was not doing anything to the first child, so the explanation must lie in something that happened to the first child...a third child hit her; her father yelled at her mother the night before; she is having a bad hair day; it really doesn't matter what.

Alternatively, the explanation could lie with the second child. He could've done something to the first child previously...hit her, took a toy, again the specifics don't matter. Or the explanation could lie outside the two children. For instance, the first child could be inflamed by a violent TV show. If the observer has an ax to grind, he will attach a specific interpretation to the act, but if he is observing objectively, he will acknowledge a range of possible interpretations and will investigate rather than jump to conclusions.

Now, however, let's switch perspectives. Instead of being seen by an objective observer, let's say that it happens to you. You are the child being hit in the sandbox. Now the universe of possible interpretations both shrinks and become sharply biased by what you bring to the event. For instance, if you just saw that you were hit for no reason, the conclusion you drew would necessarily be something like - the sandbox is a dangerous place or other kids can't be trusted.

However, if, depending on your self-image, you brought a negative predisposition to the situation, you could arrive at a very different and much more corrosive conclusion. In fact, you could jump to the conclusion that there is something wrong with you, something that you do not know about, but that the other kid saw and which prompted her to hit you - deservedly. If this seems far-fetched, think again. As a psychotherapist, I have seen that most of us go through life laboring under the assumption that there is something wrong with us, defending against being found out and compensating for this belief with all sorts of irrational thoughts and behaviors.

Now this prior belief that "there is something wrong with me" can also be seen as a remembered conclusion, which shapes my interpretation of being hit (deservedly), and which in turn, will shape my future interpretation of related events.

So we see that not only do we remember the events of our lives in the form of conclusions, but these conclusions were in turn derived from prior conclusions. What is more, the conclusions that we are currently forming, are forming the context by which future events will be interpreted. Thus, arises a never ending chain of internal evolution!

Let us go deeper in our examination of the nature of memory and further explore the relationship between memory and conclusion. But in order to avoid becoming too abstract, I'm going to tell you two stories about how remembered conclusions worked to form present consciousness, and how in turn, present consciousness worked to form subsequent remembered conclusions. The first story is a story about the body, about how allergies are formed. The second story is about the mind, about how a dysfunctional personality is formed.

A story about a body

Once upon a time an infant was fed cream of wheat with milk and sugar. This infant happened to have gluten intolerance, that is, he couldn't digest grains like wheat that have the protein gluten. So every time he ate cream of wheat he got sick. Now the body sickens from a specific thing, in this case gluten, but the body/mind is not so specific. It doesn't learn that it is gluten that makes the body sick. It just learns that it was cream of wheat with milk and sugar. So by and by the body/mind starts to recognize and reject cream of wheat, even before it has time to digest it. In other words, the body/mind forms an allergy (which can include wheat in general and perhaps milk and sugar as well).

Now, every time the infant eats wheat, allergic alarm bells go off, and she has an allergic reaction - crying, diarrhea, gas, what have you. Any animal will avoid eating again what made him sick the first time. Left to his own devices the infant would stop eating wheat altogether, but he isn't left to his own devices. His mother, who has been told that wheat is the staff of life, is seduced by the picture on the box of a deliriously happy baby spooning down cream of wheat, ignores the reality of her own, crying, spitting up, diarrheal child, and fails to make the connection between what she's feeding her baby and the effect it is having on him. Though she sees that all is not well, she thinks the problem is a defective baby; he is colicky or fussy or has digestive problems. It is all about him, not what she is doing, and certainly not what she's feeding him.

As the baby starts to resist eating the cereal, the mother starts to manipulate and pressure him into eating it. She begins by wheedling and encouraging. If she succeeds, she praises the child as if he has just won the Nobel Prize. On the other hand, should her efforts fail; she might become frustrated and angry and try to intimidate the child into eating. Either way the child's refusal to eat something (that makes him sick) takes on negative emotional significance. Eating wheat, even though it makes him sick, now is associated with love and approval; whereas, listening to his body is associated with disapproval, anger, and love withdrawal. What should have been a simple, rational learning process has become a drama, a conflict between self and other and ultimately a dilemma - do I choose sickness or love. If the child chooses love, he learns to disassociate the act of eating from its effect on his body and instead starts to eat for its effect on his emotions. He has chosen *an eating disorder*.

But there is more. The cream of wheat is not pure. It has pesticides sprayed on it when it is grown, fungicides added to it when it is stored, and preservatives added to it when it is packaged. In addition, since it is wheat separated from the bran and germ, synthetic vitamins are added to it to replace the natural vitamins that have been taken away. Next, it is cooked in an aluminum pot, boiled with polluted, fluoridated, chlorinated water, and, as I have said, served up with sugar and homogenized, pasteurized cows' milk all of which add problems of their own. In addition, because vitamin D is destroyed in the pasteurization, synthetic vitamin D is added to the milk. So now, the cereal, which is making the child sick and which he is developing an allergy to, is served up as a stew of pesticides, fungicides, preservatives, synthetic vitamins, aluminum, chlorine, refined sugar, and homogenized, pasteurized cows' milk (which in and of itself is indigestible and vies with wheat for the dubious honor of being the most common originator of food allergies).

Psychology teaches us that learning proceeds by association. So when all of these ingredients are eaten with an allergen and associated with the allergic reaction, the body/mind connects the dots, and recognizes all of these ingredients, when eaten together, as a complex allergen. What is more, *in time it forms primary allergies to some or all of the ingredients associated with the original allergen.*

Now consider this...all of the foods, vitamins, and chemicals found in the cream of wheat are also found in other foods the child will be eating, or at least will be eating in the same meal. For instance, milk, now a primary allergen in itself will be in chocolate milk, cheese, scrambled eggs, tomato soup, puddings, lunchmeats, and a thousand other processed foods. Everything that an allergic food touches, i.e., is eaten in association with an allergen may also become an allergen. This is the way food allergies proliferate.

But this is not all. At the same time that the child is having allergic reactions to food, he is also breathing. The air contains pollens, mold spores, soot, and all manner of noxious gases from automobiles, smog and the like. It is not only what the child eats in association with an allergic reaction that can potentially become an allergy, it is anything that he assimilates or even just experiences simultaneously with the allergic reaction.

And this may be why children who start out with wheat and milk allergies or intolerances, become allergic to vitamins, eggs, chocolate, and eventually pollens, mold spores, and gasoline fumes. It also explains how people can progress from simple food intolerances to becoming so chemically sensitive that they have to live in controlled environments. (There are, no doubt, other genetic and environmental factors as well.)

So how does this relate to the formation of remembered conclusions? An allergy is a memory/conclusion. First, a food or a component of a food makes you sick. Second, your body/mind learns that fact and subsequently tries to reject that food instead of assimilating it. Now this allergen becomes the context in which you receive (eat) subsequent foods or meals that contain it. All subsequent foods or meals that contain the allergen are associated with an allergic reaction and are potentially interpreted by the body/mind as having played a role in the allergic reaction. These are, therefore, in danger of becoming allergens themselves.

This, then, is the story of how a healthy body becomes an allergic body through the "normal" process of learning what substances to avoid and/or, when avoidance is impossible, reject.

A story about a mind

Let me tell you another story, this one about a mind. When I was in graduate school at NYU in the early 1960s, New York City experienced a blackout. Numerous stories came out of that blackout, but this is one of the most interesting. A woman had a hairdryer with a frayed cord. She was worried about using it, but her hair was wet so she used it anyhow. But this time, the instant she plugged it in, New York went black! Such is the power of association that she jumped to the conclusion that her hairdryer had blown the city's fuse. Fortunately, she confessed to the police who set her straight, otherwise she might be still telling her grandchildren about the time she blacked out New York City.

Now let us analyze what happened. What did she remember; what did those memories have to do with her perceptions at the time; what conclusions did she draw from what happened; what alternate conclusions could she have drawn; and how did the conclusions drawn effect subsequent actions. All of these questions have bearing on our understanding of the way memory works.

All that actually happened is that she plugged in her hairdryer at the same moment New York City blacked out. However, she perceived a causal relationship between what she did and what happened and concluded that her hairdryer did it. In other words, she did not really remember what *objectively* happened, i.e., that she plugged in her hairdryer and the lights went out. Rather, she remembered the conclusion that she came to.

So we see, once again, that a formative memory is not merely an objective record of what happened, like a snapshot, but rather a memory of a conclusion that has been reached.

The picture, however, is even more complicated than this. The woman also felt guilty for plugging in the defective hairdryer. In fact, it confirmed her self-image of being irresponsible (that she got from her father). What she remembered, then, is not only that she had plugged in her hairdryer the same time that New York blacked out, or even, that she had blacked out New York by plugging in her defective hairdryer. No, she also remembered that she was still an irresponsible child - and just as her father had foretold, it finally had gotten her into big, big trouble – furthermore, she had better confess, because if she was found out before confessing, the punishment would be even worse!

As complex as this is, it becomes even more so if you reflect that if she didn't already feel guilty, she probably wouldn't have come to the conclusion that her hairdryer blacked out New York in the first place.

All of which illustrates my point that memories are not static pictures. They are conclusions, set up by prior conclusions, which in turn play an active role in forming future conclusions.

The chain of events didn't stop there, however, because the woman's next action was to confess her wrongdoing to the police. The police, of course, reassured her and sent her home. But they also laughed at her, which compounded her embarrassment and made her feel silly. Thus, they corrected her conclusion, which effectively cleared the memory. However, in correcting the conclusion, they replaced it with another conclusion. Now she remembered making an embarrassing mistake and concluded that not only was she irresponsible, she was silly as well...w*hich she might have been, but only because she spent much of her life living up to or living down a self-image of being irresponsible.*

Memories are overlaid with other memories all the time. When negative memories become overlaid with positive memories, that is a therapeutic process. It is constructive education. However, when they are overlaid with other negative memories, it is a destructive process. It is particularly destructive when negative memories build on a prior negative self-image, which is usually the case.

So to remember, *a memory is not only what we remember, it is also what we conclude.* The conclusion of being irresponsible created the further conclusion of blacking out New York, which in turn created the further conclusion of being silly.

Deconstructing chains of associated conclusions

These examples provide an understanding of the way perceptual contexts are built up and in turn, suggest a strategy by which they can be broken down again. This is the process of Psychonoetic Clearing. If the formative memory of being irresponsible had been cleared prior to the New York blackout, then that entire, embarrassing incident (which led to the further conclusion of being silly) would never have happened, and instead, life would've provided our protagonist with just another occasion for cosmic laughter.

That which we have concluded becomes part of what we are. At the same time, what (we think) we are, in turn, effects what we become in the future. Even now, the sum of all of your past conclusions is invisibly shaping your interpretation of present events. This is how character determines fate.

It follows, then, that if the conclusions we have drawn for ourselves are erroneous, they will falsify our perceptions, misdirect our actions and perpetrate dysfunctional patterns. In other words, they will create negative consequences or what the East calls negative karma. Negative karma, in this view, is comprised of the effects or implications of incorrect conclusions rather than the workings of an intrinsic law of the universe or divine judgment and retribution.

An incorrect conclusion is false, and clearing it is a return to truth. All formative memories are, first and foremost, conclusions about the nature of oneself. (Actually it is difficult to imagine what a conclusion that is not about oneself could possibly be, since every conclusion about the world or *not self* implies something about self.) And of course, it is easy to see how any idea, mistaken or not, about who or what one is, will have consequences. If what we think we are is really the sum of our conclusions, then it is reversible. It can be changed. It doesn't have to be atoned for by suffering. The truth can change it, the very same truth that Jesus referred to when He said, "The truth shall set you free."

This is a subtle and very important statement. It is also very easy to misconstrue. Psychonoetic Clearing does not convey truth! It does not convey anything. It just clears the debris away. The truth is already within us! The truth is only clear perception.

Conversely, it is only our distorted viewpoint that keeps us from seeing what is true, and it is only attachment to the same distorted viewpoint that keeps us from accepting what is true. PsychoNoetics releases the erroneous conclusions that are tantamount to a distorted viewpoint - and the clearing, in turn, allows us to perceive and accept reality from the vantage point of who we really are!

Chapter 6
PsychoNoetics: The Science of Identity

PsychoNoetics is a science and an art. It is the science of identity, the study of how identity works on the physical, psychological, and spiritual levels as the kingpin of the whole person. At the same time it is an art, the art of identity management. Psychonoetic techniques concern themselves with how identities and their underlying memories and conclusions can be seen, evaluated, cleared, and revised.

Identities: who we are
Why has identity become the central principle of my work? Our identities are who we are - on all levels. Your body is your identity. Your personality is your identity. The way you look to yourself is your identity. The roles you play in your life are - or at least can be – identities. Your religion, your nationality, your home team, your company, all of these, if you identify with them, can be your identities. Anything that you identify with

becomes an identity. Correspondingly, anything that you dis-identify with, even your body, stops being your identity.)

However, the root of all identities, both evolutionarily and in the present lifetime, is the *physical body*. When we identify with our bodies, we identify with a living, biological organism, a vulnerable, physical *thing*. Our bodies are fragile. They are dependent on oxygen, water, food, warmth, and shelter. What is more, they are vulnerable to attack from toxins, bacteria, viruses, fungi, animals, and other humans. Our bodies can get sick or old and die. They have to eat, and they can be eaten.

Because of this root identity as a physical body, we are constantly in survival mode as the bottom line of our existence. Survival mode has two broad aspects, *making a living* and *defense*. Making a living includes all those aspects of getting what we need to survive, procreate, and thrive—food, clothing, shelter, attracting a mate, etc.—in whatever ways are appropriate to the environment and society we live in. Defense, on the other hand, comprises all those ways in which we protect ourselves. Basically, we protect our bodies from being killed, being eaten and being damaged by the substances that we incorporate, whether through breathing, ingesting, or absorbing through the skin.

However, and this is really the point, because our identity as a mortal, physical body is the paradigm for all of our identities, we have an irresistible tendency to defend our psychological and social identities as if they are our body. This is true whether they are our self-concepts, our roles, our self-esteem, our religion, or even our home team - any threat to them, however trivial, seems life threatening.

If, as we advance in "spiritual"understanding, we disidentify from our physical bodies and increasingly identify with our immaterial or spiritual bodies, the hold that survival fear has upon us lessens, and the advent of a "higher" identity creates different interpretations and different social choices.

Defending an identity

Let me give you an example. When Jill was a young girl, she attended a small country school in which she excelled effortlessly and always led the class. Her teachers and parents all made much of her, praising not only her performance, but also the fact that she was so smart that she didn't even have to study. In time "smarter than" became her identity.

When Jill got older, however, and went to a central high school she encountered more competition. For first the first time in her life she had to work to get good grades. She could still get them, but getting them by studying didn't count, it didn't validate her identity. Worse yet, it put it at risk, for if she worked hard and didn't get the grades, she wasn't as great as she fancied herself to be. Defending her identity, then, enmeshed her in a double bind.

Rationally, it's better to give up an imaginary superiority for a realistic success. But to an emotionally insecure person, this might not seem true. While buckling down to work was the only reasonable option for Jill, people are not always reasonable, particularly when caught in a double bind. Only by not studying and still getting good grades could Jill validate her identity as "smarter than ", and unfortunately that was not in the cards.

Negative and positive identities

"Smarter than" or any superior identity is a positive compensation, but when Jill refused to put her intelligence to the test, she was also defending against an implicit and denied negative identity. It was not "dumber than" because that was not Jill's particular problem. Rather it was something like "less popular than" or "less lovable than".

Everywhere we find a positive identity, we also find a negative one for which it is compensating. And of course, the corollary is true; everywhere we find a negative identity, we can be sure there is a compensatory positive identity somewhere out there!

For instance, if a young man started out with a negative identity as a coward and a weakling, he would generate a wish to be strong and fearless which he would then attempt to turn into an identity, perhaps by lifting weights or learning karate. On the other hand, he might compensate by trying to make a lot of money, or playing the guitar, or writing poetry and being sensitive. Whatever compensatory identity he found would be defended with greater intensity than someone who found that same identity without it being a compensation.

Whenever we encounter a positive identity that also has an aspect of superiority, we can suspect that a negative identity with feelings of inferiority lurks beneath.

Whatever we are defending, it is always an identity. This is the bottom line.

So, whether you are in a physical identity (allergy) or a psychological one, it is still an identity. And whenever you are in identity and that identity is challenged, you're going to defend yourself, and your body is going to prepare for that defense with a fight or flight reaction. This is the bottom line.

As I have said, when we defend ourselves on any level, physical or psychological, we are fundamentally defending our body. Our bodies know that, and they respond to all threats as mortal threats, whether they are an allergen, an automobile accident, or an insult! If a threat is resolved reasonably quickly, whether you win or lose, it is just going to be a momentary struggle. However, if it is not resolved, if the threat is on-going or chronic, your body is going to sustain an adrenaline reaction over a long time. That is the kind of stress that breaks you down and makes you ill.

Stress

An excellent indicator that we have unconscious stuff that needs to be cleared is the presence of stress in our daily lives. When we feel "stressed out", we can be reasonably sure that some deep memories, physical or psychological, are playing themselves out on the screen of our mind. There are many things, from yoga to a stiff drink that can lower our stress, but all of them are temporary and lead to dependency. Psychonoetic clearing does much more; it helps us let go of the memories and therefore the identities that create the stress in our daily lives, thus heading it off before it arises.

Stress syndrome

All stress is a defensive reaction; as I maintained above, it is the defense of our identity, physical or ideation. Stress syndrome is more than that; it is a partial or total breakdown caused by continual stress. When the fight or flight reaction of the sympathetic nervous system is continually activated, our system becomes exhausted and starts to break down.

When does this happen? It happens when there is no possible way of terminating the threat that is creating the stress. In other words, as long as the danger remains constant, the body remains in a state of defensive arousal, and when this situation becomes chronic, stress syndrome ensues.

Most real dangers are sharply circumscribed. When an antelope is being chased by a lion, it either escapes or is eaten. Either way the situation is quickly resolved.

However, when threats are self-generated, when circumstances threaten us because we are holding onto identities, they cannot be resolved. The threat comes from within us, is rooted in our own ideas about ourselves, and we find ourselves being "threatened" again and again throughout our day from circumstances that are not actually about our physical survival. (We all know people whose external circumstances are enviable, who are subject to little or no visible threat, yet who are continually "stressed out". Their threats are self-generated.)

This constant defensiveness creates a continual state of stress, and continual stress turns into that which physicians and psychologists call stress syndrome. From stress syndrome comes a cascade of physical and psychological symptoms and can, in extreme cases, cause a complete breakdown of health. Allergies, autoimmune disorders, and all manner of metabolic and systemic disturbances can be traced to the chronic defense of false physical identities, just as *the majority of psychological disturbances* can be traced to the defense of false psychological identities.

False identities are revealed through allergic and emotional reactions

As we experience our lives we create an unconscious network of conclusions about ourselves and our world. These conclusions imprison us with glass walls. The walls are invisible, but whenever we are unexpectedly thrown into reaction, we fly into them and it hurts.

When the body's memories of physical illness or pain trigger the immune system, we slam into the walls of an allergic reaction. *An allergic reaction is a physiological defense mechanism.* It is the body trying to defend itself against, or rid itself of a substance that it recognizes as incompatible. The body is, in effect, defending a boundary of self/not self, which it has learned through past experience.

When the mind's memories of emotional pain trigger the ego, we slam into the walls of an emotional reaction. *An emotional reaction is a psychological defense mechanism.* It is the body/mind trying to defend its ideas about itself in the face of circumstances that it recognizes as incompatible with those ideas. The body/mind is in effect defending a boundary of self/not self, or identity, which it has learned through past experience.

These boundaries first formed in the past, as we interacted with people and things and formed self-concepts, both physiologically and psychologically. However, we are always engaged in this process, continually refining what we "know" about ourselves and our world. Some of these self-concepts fall by the wayside, usually for lack of reinforcement, but others stay with us. Either they are repeatedly reinforced, or the circumstances in which they have been learned are dramatic or traumatic. When our self-concepts achieve permanent status, they become our *identities*, and they make us vulnerable. And, as I said, when we take on an identity, we become obliged to *defend* it.

One interacting system to defend

In some ways we can envision our body/mind and the entirety of our defensive structure, as one interacting system. In this system, allergies are aggravated by emotions, and emotions are impacted by our physical state of being. Our immunological, hormonal, and nervous systems are constantly sharing information about what we know about ourselves as a whole, and how best to defend our self-defined boundaries.

This is the system we are called upon to defend. But when perceived threat is constant, defense is constant. And constant defense cannot be maintained without the creation of a resultant stress syndrome and its concomitant breakdown of body and mind. We must find ways to stop the cycle of creating false or unnecessary, inner boundaries, and then defending them as if our physical survival was at stake.

Releasing us from the loop of self-generated threats

If we understand that every reaction is a communication to us about how we have self-defined or identified ourselves, we start to notice when and where that definition is useful. When we step off the curb, and jump back from the on-coming car that narrowly misses our nose, we can be grateful that we have an unconscious reaction to protect our body. But when a saleslady speaks brusquely, and we "lose it" in the middle of Macy's, we might want to seriously question our unconscious definition of self.

By monitoring ourselves and our reactivity this way, we gain perspective on the system of beliefs and identities by which we define ourselves. The learned boundaries that we defend are self-generated, and in this sense, all the threats that we perceive to them are also self-generated. If we understand this, we can choose to examine the boundaries of our identities, and if it seems appropriate, change them.

There are three possible ways of handling self-generated threats; avoiding the situations that create them, reducing a response to them (through drugs, exercise, meditation or the like) or clearing the memories that activate them. As to the first option, it is almost impossible to avoid all situations, physical and psychological, that trigger us. Not only is it impossible, but the attempt to do so will constrict our lives, often to an intolerable degree. As for the second option, these tools work at least partially, but they create dependencies.

It is only the third option, clearing the memories that form the boundaries of our identities, that works permanently and has no disadvantages. *This is the conscious way, the psychonoetic way, of alleviating stress.* However, most people, even in the mental health professions, are unaware of both the possibility of clearing memories and the techniques of doing so.

Summary

External threats continually arrive in life and are dealt with and forgotten. However, oftentimes threats are not real, but a product of misinterpretations, whether physical or psychological. In these cases, we are continually generating our own threats through our perceptual distortions. We can never mount an adequate defense to these threats (and thus end them), because we continually create them. Instead, we remain caught in an endless loop of threat and defense, a state which leads to the psychological and adrenal exhaustion of stress syndrome.

By clearing memories, we correct our perceptions and prevent them from creating a stress response. In these circumstances *psychonoetic memory release* can eliminate stress at its source, not only improving the quality of our lives, but also forestalling the development of chronic and debilitating illnesses.

PsychoNoetics uses simple and powerful techniques for alleviating both physical and psychological stress. However, it does this, not by weakening the normal defense mechanisms (like antihistamines, anti-inflammatory drugs, and tranquilizers in medicine) or overlaying defense mechanisms (with relaxation exercises, assurances, affirmations, and positive thinking in counseling psychology), but by identifying and deconstructing the limiting identities that we hold, so that there is no longer any boundary or false identity to defend. This is true identity management.

Chapter 7
The Clearing Path

When I first started using the emotional clearing techniques that developed into PsychoNoetics, I had specific, self-therapy goals in mind: dealing with my nervousness before a speaking engagement, getting over a fear of flying, mastering my anger, letting go of inferiority/superiority feelings, or just clearing emotional upsets as they arose.   However, as I cleared memories, thoughts, and feelings, a pattern began to emerge. I could see that I was not merely dealing with isolated thought forms, but that every clearing that I did deconstructed another facet of one unitary system, and that system was my Ego or egoic identity. And as we all know, just about every "spiritual"system identifies the ego as the enemy of awakening.

At the same time that I was developing PsychoNoetics, I was engaged in deep nondual inquiry, a spiritual path similar to the direct or steep path of Advaita Vedanta.   Classical Advaita practice is a contemplation of the question "who am I?", a contemplation that takes one deep into the nature of Self.   My path started with a different question, namely, "what is duality?" Though different, my question also pointed me toward the nature of Self, and at the same time into the role of perception in constructing our experience. (The fruits of this investigation can be found in my book <u>Oneness Perceived</u>).

Twin identities

Part of what I realized from my question about duality is that we have a twin identity, a personal one, which in some sense is illusory or false, and a universal one, which in the same sense is real or true. Our false identity is "thingness". Bodies, brains, and personalities are things, and when we identify our beingness with them, our identity is also a thing.

As things, particularly living things, we are destructible. We can get sick, and we can die. We can even be killed and eaten, and while this doesn't happen often in the modern world, it is firmly in the human racial memory and forms the emotional or symbolic substrate of much of our economic life.

Our true identity is that we are just consciousness. As consciousness we are indestructible no-things. In fact, we are immortal. Each of us is an individualized center of One consciousness, as similar to one another and as different as waves on the ocean. Of course, my center is attached to my body, but this is just a temporary attachment. As consciousness, I can be detached from my body, as in death, and reborn as another body.

Your center of consciousness is both different from mine and identical. It is different because it is attached to your body and remembers your history, but it is identical in the essence of beingness. I call this common denominator of consciousness God, and its personal realization, God consciousness. (Of course I don't expect everyone to agree with me on this.) To the extent that we align our egos with this consciousness, we have realized God consciousness and become enlightened.

A balanced role for ego

However, note that the illusoriness or realness of these twin identities is determined by where we start off in consciousness. Most of us start off in our personal identities. When we discover a more comprehensive identity underlying it, it appears that we have discovered our real identity, and consequently, that our original identity was false. However, if we are born awakened, as some of us have been, and subsequently discovered that we have a personal identity, with feelings, bodily needs, and all the rest...and that we have a need for ego boundaries...then the awakened identity would seem false, and the newly discovered, egoic identity would seem real!

This is a very important point. Prophets and spiritual teachers of all traditions emphasize the need to transcend the ego and realize universal identity, undoubtedly because they see that people have their egoic identities down pat, but are clueless when it comes to their universal identity. However, when people attempt to go to universal identity whole hog, when they attempt to live in a state of blissful, unstructured consciousness 24/7, things have gone too far in the other direction.

Both the egoic and egoless identities are true, which means that if we try to ignore one or the other of them, both are false. We need to strike a balance. Unreality and illusion cut both ways. Ignoring the ordinary world and our ordinary selves is as much an error as is ignoring our identity with God consciousness. Both are fanaticism, and both have pernicious effects.

History is full of examples of the destructive nature of unchecked ego, but it also gives us some powerful examples of the opposite extreme, like those Hindu fakirs who stare at the sun until they burn their eyeballs out, or the Buddhist theocracy of Tibet that found itself helpless before the egoic Revolution of China.

But our time here in the West gives us the best example of the denial of the ego. Here, hundreds of thousands of people, some of the best and the brightest and certainly the nicest, are in the grips of a spiritual reaction. In so far as these seekers absent themselves from the arena of power, they leave the reins of authority firmly in the grip of those who are firmly in the grip of their egos.

Identity and survival

Since our body is a thing, every identity that is derived from it is a thing as well. Moreover identifying yourself with a thing, whether it is a body, a mind, an immortal soul, or an essential self, is a philosophical and spiritual error. What is more, it is an error that needs to be transcended in order to clear the way for awakening, transformation, and enlightenment.

By definition, things are separate. In fact, *separation is the essence of thingness.* It is our felt thingness that blocks us from apprehending our universal connectivity or Oneness. Since it is our identification with our bodies as things that vitalizes all our other identities, it would seem logical to first let go of this identification. However, clearing your identification with your body could undermine your motivation to survive (as a physical being), and you should not attempt it on your own. Instead, strive to make identification with your body or, in fact, with any thing at all, light - as light as possible. You can do that by understanding "thingness", and by clearing your false identities as they come up.

Still mind

In my meditative practice I discovered that we can experience this consciousness that is our nature by going to *still mind* (a completely undisturbed and awake state of awareness). Whenever our mind is contentless, without perceptions or thoughts, and motionless and timeless, not doing, not emoting and not agitated, we are tasting consciousness, our consciousness. This state of awareness is also called being awake, being present, and being in Buddha mind - among other things. (In addition, when we go further into still mind, so that the split between witnesser and witnessed disappears, we are God and we are enlightened.)

When I realized that the portal to enlightenment is just relaxing into a still mind, I started going to still mind directly (by consciously suspending my thought processes). Once there,

I attempted to stay there and function from it. However, as anyone who has attempted a spiritual path, any spiritual path whatsoever, will tell you, understanding and even going to still mind is relatively easy, but staying there, particularly in the hurley burley of everyday life, is almost impossible.

I experimented with all of the traditional spiritual practices like meditation and yoga, but while these practices were effective in moving me to still mind, I found them almost useless when it came to staying there deliberately when facing any kind of threat. This was equally the case, whether the threat was real and external, or just "in my mind". And so I started looking for ways to safeguard my still mind.

The Clearing Path

Gradually, it dawned on me that what I was looking for in the spiritual realm, I was already developing in PsychoNoetics. Meditative and yogic practices stilled my mind, but they didn't keep it still. Sooner or later my mind, in dialogue with the outside world, would call me back. PsychoNoetics also got me into a still mind, but it did it differently. It eased me in by clearing away the memories, beliefs, attachments, and the like which distracted me in the first place. Unlike the fleeting centeredness afforded by meditation and yoga, which are essentially repetitive practices, the effects of psychonoetic letting go were relatively permanent. As I stripped away aspects of my false identity, I had less left to defend - and therefore less could upset me.

Each clearing that I did, undid a conclusion about myself that was either false on the outset or no longer applicable. (Each conclusion had been part and parcel of a false or egoic identity, and each time these conclusions were triggered, they disturbed my still mind.) As I progressed in my clearing practice, my false identity started to break up, like sheet ice melting in the sun, and the clear, still water of my real identity started to shine through.

99

So gradually I understood that my right hand was working on the same project as my left one. The psychonoetic techniques I was developing for healing and psychotherapy, were more than therapeutic techniques; they were, or could be, a spiritual path in and of themselves. They were not only the means of getting in touch with that portal to real identity, the still mind; they were also the means to safeguard and even deepen it. Furthermore, they did this, not by soothing my emotions or suppressing my thoughts and desires, but by clearing them, false conclusion after false conclusion, finally leaving nothing that was not aligned with my true identity.

In this way, PsychoNoetics aligned with spiritual inquiry and realization, creating a monastery without walls, a garden of stillness, which first safeguarded my identity and then became it. I came to call this joining of PsychoNoetics and nondual inquiry the *Clearing Path*. I invite you to walk it with me.

Chapter 8
The Basic Steps in a Psychonoetic Clearing

What is a psychonoetic clearing?
We can all identify those areas of our lives that we wish would go away...some feelings, some situations, some stress. We have been educated to believe that these problems are part of us, or at best that they can only be fixed by a psychologist or medicated into submission. Psychonoetic clearing is a way of letting go of these problems by restructuring the psyche that creates or projects them. Once mastered, it is a relatively simple process. However, mastering the process in itself requires not only work, but also a certain degree of self-transformation.

There are four phases to a psychonoetic clearing:
- *Preparation*
- *Playing 20 questions*
- *Testing*
- *Clearing*

Preparation

Whether you are doing PsychoNoetics on your own or with help in a therapeutic situation, the first step is to prepare yourself. Preparation is simply getting present, and getting present connects you to the psychonoetic dimension. The practices we use, like balanced posture, following your breathing, and concentration will be familiar to many readers. They are variations on practices common to many transformational disciplines. They work. However, if you are already on a meditative path and have your own practices, by all means feel free to use them. Any practice that gets you present will do.

Playing 20 questions with God

Psychonoetic investigation is a process of asking *yes-or-no* questions, and doing auto-kinesiological testing to get answers. There are various ways you can question any of your unconscious parts and get an answer. We will go into them extensively in the following pages. For now just know that you can question any part of your body and mind. You can even ask your higher Self or universal consciousness for various sorts of guidance.

Perhaps you have played the parlor game of 20 questions. In the days of black and white TV there was a game show of that name. Somebody thinks of something, the more improbable the better, and then tells it to the audience, but not to the panel. The point of the game, of course, is for the panel to guess what it is. They have 20 questions in which to zero in on the answer. The limitation, however, is that their questions can only be answered *yes* or *no*! This means, of course, that they have to formulate their questions thoughtfully.

Twenty questions is a strategic game. Bad players guess wildly until they run out of chances. Good players halve the universe of possibilities with each question until the answer drops into their lap. Great players halve the universe with each question and at the same time intuitively tune in the answer. When we play *20 questions with God,* this is what we are doing - asking *yes-or-no* questions and zeroing in on the answer. We start with strategy, and in time *intuition develops.*

Testing, getting to yes

Testing is almost a mechanical process, and yet it is also miraculous. It is the way we communicate with the God principle. The testing techniques of psychonoetic clearing are auto-kinesiological, that is, they are derived from the kinesiological art of muscle testing, but they are done very differently. Most of what we do in psychonoetic clearing is finger testing, that is, we use our fingers as a surrogate for all of the muscles that an applied kinesiologist would test. In this way we can test others without their participation, indeed without even their presence. At the same time we can test ourselves without assistance from anyone else.

Clearing

After we identify what the problem is, we can ask our subconscious to let go of it. What is released is always some form of unconscious conclusion, a memory, belief, or some such thing. Remember that even cells and organs have both consciousness and simple perceptions. What we are always doing when we clear is letting go of a mistaken or outdated conclusion of our body or our mind, therefore correcting a misperception. Mistaken conclusions lead to errors in perception and action.

Chapter 9
Step 1. Preparation

Every minute presence

In Buddhist circles, having a still mind is also referred to as *every minute Zen* or simply *mindfulness*. Others refer to it as *being in the now* or *centered*. I like to refer to this vital state of awareness as *every minute presence*, or just *presence*.

Being present or *presence* requires a "deep acceptance of *what is*". When we are not present, it is because we are running away, running away from what is happening at the present, running away from *what is*. "Running away" is just another way to say not accepting or denying. When we are not accepting, we are in the thing that we want to believe or the experience that we want to have rather than in the present. Clearing is a way of getting present and staying that way for the long-term.

But, and this is a paradox, before you can ask questions in any meaningful way, before you can clear memories, you must get present for the moment. Most of us, most of the time, are not present. In fact, we are anything but. Instead, we are agitated, rushed, anxious, busy solving problems, or otherwise distracted. As we become proficient in our clearing practice, it will become easier and easier to get present. In fact, psychonoetic clearing both moves us towards this state of uninterrupted awareness and makes it easier for us to sustain it.

As you advance in the clearing practice, you start to monitor your *every minute presence* and use any deviation from it as an indication that you have something to clear. However, in the learning stages of PsychoNoetics, it is best for most people to take the time and make it a practice to get present at the start of every clearing session.

Posture

There are three, equally important aids to presence: posture, breath, and a relaxed, empty mind. The basic posture of presence is sitting erect, either on the floor or in a straight-backed chair without leaning back. Relax your back and sit balanced on your sit bones, those little boney points in your buttocks. Then, imagine a cord attached to the center of the top of your skull and suspending you from the ceiling.

This is the basic sitting posture, and it is easiest to attain it sitting in a hard chair (never leaning back). Once you get the posture, you can practice standing up, walking around, and even sitting on the floor - without changing it. One of the great discoveries of the meditative traditions is that holding the right posture facilitates both relaxation and concentration.

Breathing

You don't have to do anything but breathe naturally and pay attention to your breathing. However, if you are distracted or agitated, deep, deliberate, conscious abdominal breathing, combined with right posture, will center you and get you present very quickly. If you are having difficulty settling down, try this breathing exercise...

Breathe like water

Breathe in slowly, imagining that the air you are taking in has the weight and consistency of water. Let that heavy air sink and fill your body from the deepest part of your abdomen and keep inhaling until your lungs are completely full. Then, using your stomach muscles, gently and slowly force the air out again. Take at least three sets of four breathes like this, then go back to breathing naturally, but consciously, mindful of your breath. If you are adept at yoga or any other meditation practice, feel free to substitute the breath-centering technique of your choice.

Relaxed, empty mind

Conscious posture and conscious breathing are going to concentrate your mind. However, it will be helpful to intentionally concentrate on something you are doing as well. One technique that I use is *listening to the silence*. In this technique you tune into your consciousness by listening to your inner silence. Just go into your inner silence and listen.

Interestingly, you do not need external quiet in order to listen to your inner silence. This inner silence is not really absence of noise; it is absence of all mental activity. Paradoxically, it is when you are in noisy, chaotic surroundings or you are agitated and chaotic inside, that listening to your inner silence is most important and most helpful. You'll find this surprisingly easy to do if you avoid one common pitfall - that of simultaneously trying to function in chaos. If we try to communicate in noisy, chaotic surroundings, we will get entrained and find it impossible to listen to our inner silence. The strategy of choice is to suspend all effortful activity and go inside where your inner silence always is!

Do it now!

Remember these are just three of many techniques that you can use. The important things in becoming present are to become conscious and stop your mind from distracting you. As you develop facility in PsychoNoetics, you will find it easier and easier to get present, but for now take a little time to do it right - prepare!

Chapter 10
Step 2. Questioning

Once we come to rest in a place of stillness, we are ready to ask questions of the psychonoetic field (Our God Self, universal consciousness, or Oneness). There are four basic kinds of questions that can be answered *yes* or *no*:

- Direct yes-or-no questions
- Multiple choice questions
- True-or-false questions
- Rating questions (on a scale, like 1 to 10)

All these questions are just variations on the yes-or-no theme, since even though the form of the question varies, the answers can always be phrased as *yes* or *no*. In fact, if you have an investigative bent, you will soon discover that you can explore in numerous ways, building on the digital framework of *yes* or *no*.

Direct yes-or-no questions

The direct yes-or-no question is very flexible. Used with skill and intuition, it can get at almost any kind of information very quickly. Basically, you play a game of Twenty Questions with God, getting *yes* or *no* answers until you zero in on the information you desire. Your success at it will depend on how well you play the game.

Twenty Questions is a game of logic where you attempt to halve the population of possibilities with each question. But it's also a game of intuition, and with practice intuition not only prompts you with the answers, but also starts to feed you the questions.

When people used to play 20 questions on television, the questioners were always given a hint. They were told whether the thing that they were trying to guess was animal, vegetable, or mineral. This limited the universe they were looking at. Then the classic first question was, "Is it larger than a bread box?" This defined size. Like these questions, your first questions should also be aimed at limiting the field of possibilities and zeroing in as much as possible. Let's say, for example, that you feel ill. You have a headache and a stomachache. Your first question should be zeroing in on what ails you:

> Am I getting sick?
> *Yes*
> Is it an infection?
> *Yes*
> Is it a bacterial infection?
> *No*
> Is it a virus infection?
> *Yes*
> Is it a cold?
> *No*
> Is it the flu?
> *No*

Is it a stomach virus?
Yes
And so on...

Multiple-choice questions

A very useful variant is the multiple-choice question. Here, you are presenting and testing a list of possibilities until you get a *yes* response on your fingers.

Take as an example a case in which you suspect that you are having an allergic response to something...

Honing in:
Am I having an allergic reaction?
Yes
Is it to something I am breathing?
No
Is it to something I ate?
Yes
Something that I ate today?
No
Something that I ate yesterday?
Yes
For lunch?
No
For dinner?
Yes

The multiple choice:
Is it the chicken?
No
The broccoli?
No
The coffee?
No
The pasta?
Yes

Am I allergic to the wheat in the pasta?
Yes

True-or-false questions

As everyone who ever took exams in high school knows, true-or-false questions are just variations on multiple-choice questions, where the choices are *true* or *false*.

Rating on a scale from 1 to 10

Let's say you want to know about something that has a continuous aspect to it, for example, your basal metabolism. Again, whatever you're investigating can be rated on a scale, such that every number of the scale is one of a series of multiple choices. I most often use a scale from 1 to 10, and then count in my mind testing at each count until I get a *yes*. I make explicit what I am requesting, and then question each possibility in the scale. Here is an example.

Give me a level from 1 to 10 on my basal metabolism. Ten would indicate a perfectly functioning metabolism for my age, height, weight, and body type. One would indicate the opposite.

One?
No
Two?
No
Three?
No
Four?
No
Five?
No
Six?
Yes

Since I discovered David Hawkins' work, I have also been using his scale for consciousness, 1 to 1000 with 1000 being the consciousness of a Buddha or Christ. I often ask myself, "How true is this statement?" and proceed to evaluate truth in hundreds (100? 200? 300? etc.), then in tens (340? 350? 360? etc.), and finally in ones (361? 362? 363? etc.). I find this to be a very useful way to evaluate the questions that I'm asking, as even small variations in how I phrase my questions (or statements) seem important. Using this scale I can hone in on the truth of a matter even when it is beyond my conscious awareness.

High-low questions

A variant on the rating question which is a little quicker and sometimes more appropriate is the high-low question. In this technique you simply ask, for example, whether your basal metabolism is high, high to moderate, moderate, moderate to low or low, testing each answer, as you would a multiple choice or number scale.

Finding years or lifetimes

Another very useful exploration is to pose a question about when in your life or evolution something happened. Here, instead of saying to yourself and questioning one through ten, you zero in on the year (or lifetime[3] if you are of this bent). The usefulness of this line of investigation is for the conscious mind.

---

[3] The beauty of this kind of investigation is that belief structures can be explored and evaluated. Many psychotherapists, myself included, have found that psychological difficulties can often be traced to past lifetimes. I have no doubt in my mind that there is a nonmaterial continuity of consciousness that transcends death, and carries information from experiences beyond the present lifetimes. However, once you "trust your fingers", I recommend that you proceed with your own investigations of this phenomenon, and open your own doorway to the immaterial realms. For me I find that this information is significant only when it is useful to uncovering one's real nature.

Issues or contractions can be cleared without any knowledge of what the problem is/was, but if we prefer to know about what happened, we can use questions and testing to obtain this kind of information. Some people find that when they know what experience initiated a false identity, they can be on the watch for other ideas that they are still holding that support and reconfirm that identity.

If you are of the need- or want-to-know variety, for economy's sake in asking questions, consider bracketing. Start with categories like birth to ten years old, ten to twenty years old, etc.; then zero in to the exact year. For those who believe in reincarnation, I often ask the question, "Did this originate in the present lifetime or a past lifetime?" without proceeding further into the details. I find that it frequently relieves the mind to hear that what it thought was an insolvable problem in this lifetime, actually is a holdover from another life's experience.

Answerable questions

I hope that it is becoming clear that there are really very few limitations on what you can investigate by asking yes-or-no questions. There are, however, some requirements that must be met for this system to produce meaningful *and true* information.

- The question has to be about something that exists now, that is in the *eternal present*. It cannot be about the future because the future doesn't exist, it is only a vector of probability. On the other hand, *it can be about the past* because the past is held in the present as memory.
- The question has to be about something in consciousness. It has to be a question whose answer is actively known, either by your consciousness, the consciousness of another, or by some overriding or universal level of consciousness. If it is not in consciousness, you cannot tune into it through your

consciousness. (Examples are the condition of a part of the body, an intention held by the mind, or even a level or quality of consciousness.)

- As much as possible, the question should refer to something real, not something that is only a matter of appearance or perception. For instance, the playing card the *ace of clubs* is not the ace of clubs in reality. It is only the ace of clubs when perceived as such by someone familiar with cards. In consciousness it just consists of fibers of wood and cotton with a pattern of black ink. So the question, *is this the ace of clubs* is unlikely to get an accurate answer. However the question, *does George perceive he has the ace of clubs in his hand*, will get an accurate answer.

A cautionary note

Note that there is a precision to asking questions of "God consciousness". The more precise you are and the more you reside in *presence,* the more effective your investigations will be. Let us consider some of the possible sources of error.

First of all, there is the obvious danger of subjectivity in auto-kinesiological testing. Briefly, whenever there is an emotional charge on a question, whenever there is an answer that *you do* or *do not want to get*, subjective distortion is a very real possibility.

Secondly, if you ask consciousness a question that It cannot answer, there is an excellent possibility that your imagination will answer, and you will get a false reading. This is related to *false memory syndrome,* and is a problem that hypnotists encounter time and time again. And just as an unanswerable question about the past can evoke a false memory syndrome, an unanswerable question about the future can evoke a *false future syndrome.*

The best way to prevent this from happening is to avoid asking questions that are exceptions to the above rules. Also, be as clear and unambiguous as possible in the phrasing of questions. The unconscious is very literal, and if the question can be misinterpreted, chances are the unconscious will do it.

Finally, avoid asking the same question repeatedly. Doing so will confuse your mind. In addition, asking the same question twice will reverse your finger polarities so that a *yes* response becomes a *no* response. When this happens, repeat your training questions (discussed in the next chapter) to re-establish your polarity, and then repeat your question.

Chapter 11
Step 3. Testing for Answers

After we get present and pose our question, we are ready to receive an answer. It is important to begin with the intention that any information received come from universal mind (the God principal, Oneness, or however you care to refer to it), and important to check whether any given answer does indeed emanate from this level of Source. Information can arrive in two forms: analog or digital, and each should be handled differently.

Analog answers
Analog means that the answer comes in an integrated communication, like seeing a visual image, hearing a voice, or getting a direct intuition. Some people are natural clairvoyants, they are very open to analog communications, and they get them all the time. You might wish to be able to do this; however, it is a mixed blessing for a number of reasons.

First of all, analog communications are more susceptible to the distortion of subjectivity. Among other things, what you want to hear or are afraid to hear enters very strongly into what you actually hear. Second of all, analog information needs more interpretation than digital information.

I once knew a minister who got all sorts of visions. One time he got a vision of God sitting on a throne surrounded by choirs of Angels. He himself was seated on God's right, on a throne only slightly less resplendent. What was he to make of this? On the one hand, it could be interpreted as telling him simply that his own nature is close to God nature. But on the other, the grandeur of his image of God could easily lead to grandiosity of self.

In addition to these dangers, analog communications come from various sources, some wise and benevolent, some less so. Some come from the level of consciousness associated with enlightened beings like Christ and Buddha, but others come from lower levels, some more well-meaning than wise, and others downright malevolent. The sources can be as various as internal fears, unintegrated fragments of yourself, and even perhaps, other people or entities that you are tuning into unwittingly. Only the communications from the Christ or Buddha level should be relied upon. For this reason, even if you choose to stick with analog messages for guidance, you should validate them by testing. When channeling, the first question you should ask on your fingers is, "Is this communication from the Christ or Buddha level?" If it is not, you should not only disregard it, but also shield your consciousness from it.

There's another problem with clairvoyance as well. Clairvoyants, by their nature, tend to be very open, have porous boundaries, and be susceptible to all sorts of psychic influences. This creates psychological challenges for them that we more pedestrian souls do not have to deal with. Psychonoetic testing, on the other hand, develops a different and, I believe, more manageable, intuitive channel.

Digital answers

Unless you are already prone to receiving analog communications, it is difficult to develop analog reception from scratch. On the other hand, the ability to access digital information as yes-or-no answers, is easier to develop, and with practice gives the average person a route to higher information. Furthermore, because answers consist of *yes's* or *no's*, with careful questioning, answers can be less subjective and more specific.

Even if you are not a particularly "intuitive" type, by playing the game of Twenty Questions with God you can develop amazing skill at accessing information. And, after practicing for a while, your intuition seems to grow, and you begin to know easily what questions to ask. The process becomes less a random investigation and more a matter of checking your hunches.

In PsychoNoetics, we use digital information to focus our attention on the false conclusions and subsequent identities we want to clear. We do this by asking questions, talking to ourselves, either silently or out loud, and "testing on our fingers" to receive answers. These answers are digital, not only because they come in a digital, yes-or-no form, but also because they come through our digits or fingers - a nice pun indeed!

Testing our fingers

Finger testing is auto-kinesiology. It is a variant of applied kinesiology, in which the energy state of an organ or bodily system is evaluated by testing the strength of an associated muscle.[4] Basically, a person's arm or other limb is pushed in a certain direction, while touching a trigger point or asking a question. If the arm gives way easily, i.e., the relevant muscle is "weak", that is interpreted as a blockage or weakness in the corresponding energy meridian and/or a structure supplied by that meridian.

---

[4] See *Touch for Health* by John Thies.

However, as I discussed in *The story of how PsychoNoetics was born,* I find this explanation of how kinesiology works to be only part of the story. In my own development as a psychological kinesiologist, I found myself using kinesiology to effectively answer questions that were completely unrelated to the body. I could not explain this phenomenon using the explanation of energy meridians. And as I developed PsychoNoetics, I came to rely on this ability to kinesiologically access information seemingly unrelated to the body.

Even more inconsistencies come from kinesiology itself. Some practitioners have discovered that rather than testing a client's arm, one's own muscle strength can provide information, e.g., through strength variation in the practitioner's fingers, or "finger testing". In fact, because finger testing eliminates the variables of the strength and effort of the client, it can be even more reliable than conventional kinesiological testing. Even if the information received through a practitioner's finger testing is interpreted as blockages in energy meridians, the blockage must be communicating to the practitioner through a field effect of some sort rather than through the meridians themselves. My alternate explanation is that information is available within the psychonoetic field, the One consciousness that we all are part of. Resting in this viewpoint, I use finger testing confidently as an essential part of PsychoNoetics.

Although you could test yourself by having someone press down your arm, it requires the help of another person, one who is trained. Doing the work necessary to develop finger-testing skills seems by far the most efficient route to receiving digital information.

There are various techniques by which to finger test, but they are all variants on the same principle.

Devi's Way

The technique taught to me by the founder of NAET, Devi Namburdripad, and which I still use, is called the O-ring technique. In this technique you make two circles by pressing your thumb and ring finger together and then interlace them. To test, you try to pull them gently, but firmly apart. If they come apart, that is a "yes" answer. If they don't, it is a "no". (*The polarities are strictly a convention. You can program yourself so that coming apart is a "no" answer. The important thing is to be consistent.*)

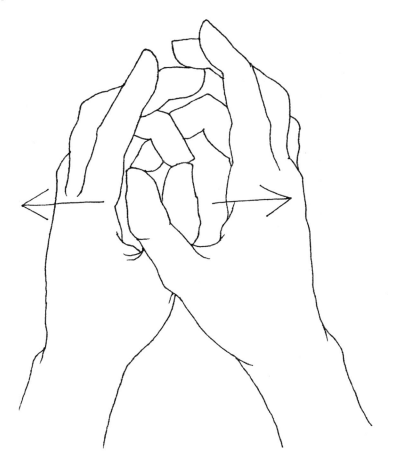

Figure 1. Devi's Way. Auto-kinesiology using the thumb-to-ring finger contact (O-ring) of one hand to test the strength of the O-ring on the other hand.

Rich's way

Richard Brightheart used a one-handed method of finger testing. He pressed his index finger down with his middle finger. This more closely parallels the act of a kinesiologist pressing down on a client's arm. This is a very elegant way of testing. It only requires one hand and is easily concealed. However, I have never mastered it.

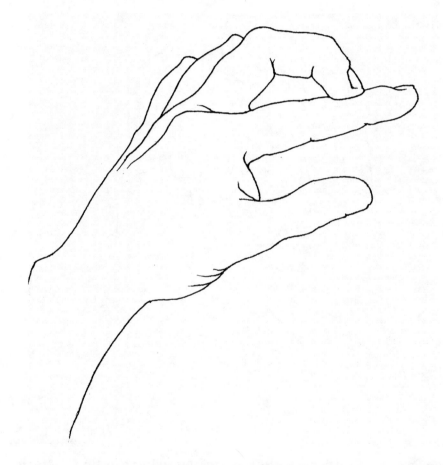

Figure 2. Rich's Way. Auto-kinesiology using the middle finger to test the strength of the index finger.

Training your fingers

Some people master finger-testing immediately, but most of us have to practice awhile before we get the hang of it. Jeanie got it immediately, but I took weeks to master it. However, now, because I practice so much, I am faster and more accurate than Jeanie. So don't get discouraged, perseverance pays.

Training your fingers and your unconscious is simpler than you may think. First, you ask yourself a question to which you know the answer, the more obvious the question, the better. My question is, "Am I a woman?" I test and when I get an answer, I then ask, "Am I a man?" You can use these questions or make up some of your own.

"Is my name Jeff?" "Is my name Jeanie?" After each of your two questions, try to pull your fingers apart, with the intention that your fingers will come apart easily to signify a "yes" answer, but stay together if the answer is "no". After awhile, your unconscious will get the message, and your fingers will start to work to give you consistent answers. Then, the sky's the limit.

If by some chance, you have already been trained in kinesiology, and use the reverse signature (strength = yes; weakness = no), don't try to re-educate yourself. Go with the polarity you know since it is already in your body. There is no right association here, only a need for consistency.

I might add that learning the entire process of psychonoetic clearing can be facilitated by working with a PsychoNoetics practitioner. It seems that the ability to establish a connection between one's fingers and one's Higher Self can be transmitted from an expert practitioner to a novice. Those of you already practiced in psychic phenomenon might try tuning into my field, and see if that helps your testing.

Maintaining polarity

Repeating your training questions is also a good technique for resetting or correcting reversed polarity. The way you set your polarities can accidentally become reversed, and your fingers can give you opposite readings, testing weak for a *no* answer and strong for a *yes* answer. In these cases, repeating the two training questions will reset the polarities. *I myself set my polarities by running through my training questions each time I start to test, and I recommend you do it as well.* It will prevent you from making many mistakes. Most kinesiological practitioners are aware of this danger, and check to make sure that their polarity is not reversed.

The way polarity typically becomes reversed is by asking the same question or a similar one twice in a row. As a matter of fact, if you test on the same question repeatedly, you will get a continual alternation of positive and negative responses. I recommend that you try it and experience it for yourself. It will definitely impress upon you the need to keep your polarities straight.

Accessing digital information the slow and sure way

The slow and sure way is to use a pendulum. The procedure is simple. Hold the pendulum in a hand which is still, but not rigid. Then say, "Show me a *yes*." Sooner or later the pendulum will establish a clear pattern of movement, clockwise, counterclockwise, or back and forth in some direction or another. Then say, "Show me a *no*." The pendulum will settle into a fixed pattern, which will be clearly different from the first pattern. In the future you can ask your questions and let the pendulum answer them by showing you one of its movement patterns. This is a very reliable method once you get the hang of it, but it also very slow.

Finding your way

Some people have devised other ways of intuitively accessing universal consciousness. Jeanie, for instance, can sense the answer to her questions without recourse to her fingers. If you start with Devi's or Rich's way of finger testing, and as you get more expert, you sense a better way for you, feel free to develop it.

Repeating the cautionary note about subjectivity

Finger testing and using the pendulum can be amazingly accurate. They can also be self-serving and inaccurate, and you can badly deceive yourself. Usually, people get wrong readings when they are emotionally invested in the outcome. If you are afraid of an answer, you will usually not get it, whether or not it is true. On the other hand, when you're intensely desirous of getting a specific answer, there's a good chance that you will get it. So when you are testing something that is very important, and have an intense emotional or even fear element associated with it, don't trust the answer you get. Check it some other way.

The trick in getting accurate readings is to be as unattached to the outcome as possible, although sometimes this is a good trick indeed. Try not paying attention to your fingers until they have done their thing; in this way you minimize your tendency to control them.

Checking subjectivity and going for truth

There are two further things you can do to minimize emotional distortion in your testing. The first is to set your intention to go for truth and not what you want to hear. You can do this by simply saying the words "go for truth" in your mind. The second is to ask yourself whether there is any subjectivity in a previous answer and then test that question.

Psychonoetic testing samples consciousness and nothing else. If it is not in consciousness, you will not be able to read it. However, there are different levels of consciousness with different contents. For example, you might be attempting to read your body and instead read your opinion. These are both completely valid readings since they are both in consciousness; however, one is useful and the other is not. When I suspect this is happening, I simply tell myself to "read my body and not my opinion".

Interestingly, I find this to be more of a problem when I'm using PsychoNoetics to read another person than when I'm reading myself. When I'm reading myself, I can sense when I'm holding a strong opinion and suspend it, but when I'm reading someone else, I have less control of the opinion field. Some people trust and flow easily, but others are very skeptical or always have a strong opinion. When I'm working with such people, I always have to be cautious not to read and confirm their opinion, but instead to "go for truth".

Even in the best circumstances, however, it is not good to rely on your fingers alone, particularly when making crucial decisions. Seeking a second, objective opinion is always prudent - particularly in matters pertaining to health, finances, or life choices. In addition, I have found that the information that I obtain by testing is seldom counterintuitive, but instead often gives me an opening where my reason and my intuition come into alignment. When I am really tuning into truth, there is kind of a "fit" where it all makes sense, a kind of "common" sense.

Chapter 12
Step 4. Letting Go of Memories

After you identify the problem by asking questions and testing for the answers, you ask your unconscious to let go or clear it. What is released always starts with a *memory*. However, there is more to it than that. Memories inevitably lead to adaptive strategies of body, mind, and action.

Body memories create allergic reactions and other physiological responses. Remember that even cells and organs have consciousness and thus have something akin to "informational" structures. The immune system in particular remembers things it experienced as toxic or associated with a toxic exposure and thus forms allergies. Psychological memories, on the other hand, lead to defensive reactions, emotional disturbances, erratic, self-destructive behaviors, and ultimately, stress syndrome.

As we release memories, and their associated psychological structures, we also release the physical and psychological states and reactions that have been built upon them.

Thus, we can begin to function completely and optimally in the present, with clear perceptions, refined emotions, and appropriate actions.

How to let go

After *preparation* and *testing*, letting go is relatively simple. You just ask yourself to do it. You *intend* it. You intend it by requesting it of yourself. That's all there is to it. You can talk to yourself out loud or silently, request yourself to let go, and it happens.

Again, however, the efficacy of your request depends upon your preparation and the state in which you are resting. You must be present and focused. For those of you who are familiar with the chakra systems, it can help to focus on your third eye (just above the midpoint of your eyebrows) or crown chakra (the very top of your head). These are energy vortices, often associated with the energy meridian system, that enhance clarity.

The last question

Before you clear, there is one, last question you always have to ask, *"Am I ready to let go of this?"* Then you finger-test. If you get a *yes* answer, proceed by saying, *"Please do so now."*

If you do not get a *yes* answer to the readiness question (and you do not always get a *yes*), you will have to find out what you're holding on to—then let that go—before you can proceed. This is beyond the scope of this chapter, but I can tell you that the process is basically the same as the primary clearing except that now you are investigating the problem that underlies the problem you started with. I ask, "Is it pinned by a memory?" and start the process of questioning all over again.

Potentiating the clearings

Sometimes the clearings work without saying anything, by simply intending to clear. With experience these times will become more frequent. However, there are techniques that are always helpful in this regard. I call them potentiating techniques.

The thinker

One of these techniques, I call *the thinker* (after the Rodin sculpture of the same name). Rodin's thinker is bending over and resting his chin on the palm of one hand, deep in thought. In Eisen's *thinker* the man is resting his forehead on his palm. What is essential is the placing of the palm on the forehead right above the eyebrows. This is the location of the chakra I referred to as the third eye. In yogic theory the third eye is the seat of psychic powers, and I have found that putting my concentration there facilitates psychonoetic clearing and testing. Although you do not have to place your hand on your third eye in order to place your concentration there, it is very helpful, particularly when you are starting out in this work, or when you're working in distracting surroundings.

Figure 3. The Thinker. Focusing attention on the third eye by placing the palm to the forehead.

TAT

A variation of the thinker is the TAT procedure[5]. It consists simply of placing your thumb and middle finger on both sides of your nose and your index finger in the center of your forehead just above the line of your eyebrows (the third eye again). This works like *the thinker* position of the palm to center your consciousness in the third eye, with the advantage of a physical focus that can powerfully facilitate psychonoetic work.

Hold the thinker or TAT position until you experience the clearing (but not more than 2 minutes). The experience of clearing ranges from an almost imperceptible shifting to an internal earthquake. Sometimes it will be experienced as a slight relaxation; other times you will not feel it at all. Occasionally, it will be accompanied by involuntary crying and spasmodic jerking movements of the spine (kriyas). How deeply you feel it depends on how sensitive you are and also on how much energy is being released by the clearing. Usually you will experience a release of internal tension, accompanied by a spontaneous, deep breath.

---

[3] I am most grateful for this procedure, which came my way with during my NAET training, but which I am no longer able to reference.

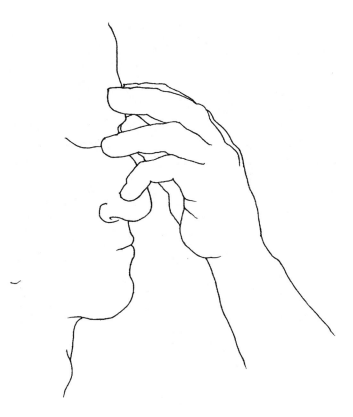

Figure 4. Focusing attention on the third eye with TAT.

Cross crawl

Another technique, one much used in a therapeutic method known as Edu-K[6], as well as by applied kinesiologists, is cross crawl. To do a cross crawl, do the following:

1. Stand on your right leg
2. Lift your left knee to about where it is level to your hip (but not higher than is comfortable).

---

[6]Edu-K or Educational Kinesiology is a system of physical movements which bring the hemispheres of the brain into balance. It was developed by Dr. Paul Dennison and Gail E. Dennison.

3. Swing your knee over to the right
4. At the same time swing your arms over to the left so that your knee and lower part of your body is moving one way and your arms and the upper part of your body is moving the opposite way.
5. Then reverse this movement so that your left knee swings towards the right and your arms swing towards the left. (Imagining yourself in a marching band helps make this movement feel very natural.)
6. Alternate this gentle "march" at a comfortable tempo for two to three minutes.

This should be adequate to potentiate a clearing.

Figure 5. Using the cross-crawl to communicate the clearing to all parts of the body-mind.

Eye movement cross crawl

Alternating eye movement is another potentiating technique that is very effective and easily used in a small space. This is a simple technique from EMDR[7], another effective strategy for releasing trauma. With your eyes closed, look alternately from your far left to your far right and back again, repeating the movement for two minutes, or until you sense an internal release.

Summary

This then is a summary of the basic psychonoetic clearing process. At its heart it is very simple (but not necessarily easy). It requires only that we know ourselves as conscious throughout our beings, center and presence ourselves as completely as we can, and begin to take responsibility for our psychological space.

---

[7] A psychological clearing technique originated by Francine Shapiro, Ph.D.

Chapter 13
Clearing the Body: Allergies

As we have seen, the negative memories we clear in PsychoNoetics are also conclusions. Each remembered conclusion holds us in fixed way of being, which is ultimately expressed as some aspect of our body/mind/spirit. When we clear, we stop holding ourselves in that way; we stop *being* our conclusions. This doesn't happen by overlaying forms or affirmations of any kind onto our conclusions, but instead by literally clearing away false and outmoded forms, so that the consciousness of body, mind, and spirit can spontaneously resume a healthy, unimpeded state of being.

This chapter describes an application of psychonoetic clearing to the body, to issues of health and wellness. However, it is important to remember that all health and wellness issues, both in their origin and their healing, encompass body, mind, and spirit, i.e., are issues for our whole way of being.

Allergies

Let's begin with how to clear allergies. This clearing, like every clearing, includes the four phases of preparation, questioning, testing, and clearing. It also relies importantly on some understandings from the NAET process, and for further clarification, I highly recommend the book, <u>Say Goodbye to Illness</u> by Devi S. Nambudripad, M.D., D.C., L. Ac., Ph.D.

The preparation for all applications of psychonoetic clearing is the same - getting present. However, severe allergy attacks, like all disturbed states of consciousness, are obstacles to getting present in themselves. As much as possible, alleviate the symptoms of the attack before doing the clearing. It's difficult to concentrate when you're sneezing or falling asleep. So, whatever is in your personal bag of tricks to combat allergic symptoms, don't hesitate to use it.

However, if you are in the throes of an allergic reaction, it may be that you are just going to have to do the best you can...sit up straight, or even stand up, concentrate, breathe, and proceed. It's possible to do it! With practice you'll find that you can do psychonoetic clearing under less than optimal circumstances.

(A useful trick for relieving allergy attacks is to alkalinize your body. The most convenient way I have found to do this is to dissolve two tablets of Alka-Seltzer gold [not the blue because the blue contains aspirin] in at least eight ounces of very cold water and drink it quickly.)

An example of questioning and testing

Set your polarities by asking your training questions. (Remember your training questions are those questions that you used in order to learn finger testing, for example, "Am I a woman? Am I a man?" See Chapter 11.) I always repeat these questions at the beginning of every testing sequence in order to make sure that the polarities are not reversed, in other words, that my finger strength or weakness is still associated with the answers I expect.

1. If you are feeling sick, and you suspect an allergy, ask:
    Am I getting sick?
    No (arrived at by testing on your fingers, see Chapter 11)
    Am I in allergic memory?
    Yes

2. If you get that you're in allergic memory, ask:
    Do you know what I am allergic to?
    Yes
    Is a contactant? (something coming in contact with my skin)
    No
    Is it an inhalant? (something that I am breathing)
    No
    Is it an ingestant? (something that I am eating or drinking)
    Yes

3. Once you zero in on the problem, refine it further by going down the list of suspects. For instance, if it is an ingestant, there are two strategies that I use together in order to track the culprit down. The first strategy is to determine when you have eaten it. Ask:
    Have I eaten it yesterday?
    No
    Have I eaten it today?
    Yes
    Have I eaten it this morning?
    No
    Have I eaten it for lunch?
    Yes

4. Once you zero in on the time, say you have eaten it around lunch time, you can proceed to the next stage of 20 Questions. Ask:
    Is it something I have drunk?
    No

Is it something I have taken in pill or capsule form?
No
Is it a solid food I have eaten?
Yes

5. OK, say that you found out the allergen was a food, and it was part of your lunch. Now you have a much smaller universe of possibilities to test. You can pursue one of two lines of inquiry with equal success. You can go through all of the foods you ate for lunch, or you can go through all food categories. However, for teaching purposes I'm going to combine both strategies. We will start with food categories. Ask:
Is it a vegetable or fruit?
No
Is it an animal food?
Yes
Is it meat, fish or poultry?
No
Is it dairy?
Yes
Is it cheese?
No
Is it milk?
Yes
Am I allergic to the protein in milk?
No
Am I allergic to the sugar or lactose in milk?
Yes

6. Since it is very common for adults to lack the enzyme necessary to digest milk sugar, you, at this point, might want to find out whether it is a true allergy or a digestive difficulty. Ask:
Can I digest milk?
No

Would a lactose digestive supplement help?
Yes
Have I also develop an allergic reaction to milk?
Yes

At this point there are two things that you have to do. Clear yourself for a milk allergy. Do not drink any milk or ingest any foods which contain fresh milk like ice cream or puddings without taking an enzyme supplement. In this way you will avoid the digestive difficulties that may reinstate the allergy.

Clearing

Letting go is relatively simple. You just ask yourself to do it. Basically, you talk to yourself. That's all there is to it. You can talk to yourself out loud or silently.

Ask:
Can I clear this allergic memory?
Yes
Please do so now!

Proceed to set the clearing by holding the thinker position, or TAT, or doing eye cross crawl (see Chapter 12). Hold the clearing position until you experience the release, but not more than 90 seconds. Again, remember that the experience of clearing varies. Sometimes you will feel a dramatic change, while other times it will just be an involuntary deep breath and a subtle release of tension. As you gain in experience you will know how your particular clearing process feels.

Combinations

Allergies frequently come in combinations. That is, you're allergic to a combination of things like, *pollen and mold spores* or *wheat and hydrogenated vegetable oil*. This results because the body is learning through association all the time (see Chapter 5). For example, recall that commercial baked goods, like cookies and crackers, often provide the context for a wheat allergic response to become associated with other potential allergens, such as hydrogenated vegetable oil. Through association the body soon "learns" that it is also allergic to hydrogenated vegetable oil.

In these cases you have to clear not only the first allergen, AND the second allergen, but also the combination in order to get good, consistent results. It sounds complicated, but the technique is easy.

1. After you have identified and cleared an allergen, ask:
   Are there any combinations?
   Yes
   Do you know what this combination is?
   Yes
   Is a contactant?
   No
   Is it an inhalant?
   No
   Is it an ingestant?
   Yes

2. Then follow the above procedure to identify and clear the second allergen.

3. Then clear the combination. Ask:
   Can you clear the combination of wheat and hydrogenated vegetable oil?
   Yes
   Please do so now.

4. Set the clearing with TAT or cross-crawl.

5. Now check for a third combination, and if you find one, repeat the procedure, clearing for the third substance and also for the combination of three. Repeat this until you get

that there are no more combinations. There are rarely more than two or three.

Allergy management

At this point, I am finding that although psychological clearings are permanent, physical clearings are not! Cleared allergies often reinstate themselves. I understand this to be because of the difference between thoughts and the material world, kind of like the difference between being angry and breaking a dish. It's easier to relinquish the anger than it is to repair the dish.

Because of this distinction, I think of allergy clearings as a way of *managing* allergies. Other modalities of allergy treatment, even NAET and desensitization shots, often have to be repeated in order to keep the body from reinstating its allergic habits. Often however, even these intractable systems of associated defense may be completely cleared. The permanence of the clearing seems to be dependent on two factors. One is the frequency of re- exposure. It is easier to clear an allergy to strawberries, which you eat infrequently, then an allergy to wheat, which you eat constantly, or an allergy to pollen, which you can't avoid breathing. The second factor is the degree of stress you are under. All stress, emotional, allergic or physical is additive. And when you are under stress, or your general level of stress rises, your allergies are slow to clear and quick to come back.

One possible explanation for the difficulty of clearing allergies is the very real need for the body to handle various toxicities and pathogens effectively. This complex system of protection and defense requires some measure of ever-ready response.

Allergies are an extension of this defensive structure, and can be distinguished as primary or secondary, depending on how truly toxic an allergen is to the body. A secondary allergen is an allergen that is learned by association with another allergy. The body/mind has only to release the association to release the secondary allergen.

A primary allergen, however, really *is* incompatible with the body. It is toxic or indigestible, pathogenic or irritating. These agents may continue to trigger reactivity in the body whenever they come on the scene, and even begin new chains of allergic association. In these cases allergy *management* is the best we can do so far.

If you have a real, genetic incompatibility, not an allergic one, something like gluten intolerance or the inability to digest lactose, it is imperative that you avoid that substance, otherwise your body will always in an unstable or toxic state of high stress, and you will lose your allergy treatments repeatedly.

Another variable in stress level and allergy management is the size of your *allergic load*. This is determined by how much of an allergen, or how many allergens we are exposed to at once. If your body is inundated by an allergen, as it is with pollen in the hay fever season, or if you are simultaneously exposed to multiple allergies, ingestants, inhalants and the like, your clearings will be much less stable.

Stress and "flipping"

Allergies are one form of stress. However, as I have said, there are other forms of stress as well: strong negative emotions, illness, injury, fatigue, and the like. When other forms of stress occur simultaneously with an allergic exposure, not only can you lose a specific clearing, you can lose all of your clearings at once and go into a severe, allergic reaction. I call this scenario "flipping"or "being flipped".

Fortunately, if you are alert to this possibility, it is easy to flip yourself back, i.e., to reinstate all of your clearings at one time, instead of laboriously doing them one by one.

1. This is the protocol to "flip back" to a state where the allergies you have previously cleared are once again cleared *en masse*. Ask:

Am I flipped? (i.e., am I allergic to many things?)
Yes
Do you know what all of them are?
Yes
Can I clear them and reinstate all of my allergy clearings?
Yes
Please do it now!

2. Set the clearing until you feel the release or for 90 seconds.

A word of caution

The above protocols are instructions in the use of the psychonoetic techniques of evaluation and clearing. They are tools of empowerment to begin the long journey of self-knowing and self-authority.

I am not giving medical advice about the treatment of allergies here. I am assuming that anyone who is awake enough to be reading this book on self-empowerment also has the awareness and common sense to research all treatment modalities and also to know when it is prudent to consult a primary health care provider and/or medical doctor. When your clearings are ineffective, the best questions to ask may be "Do I need to ask for help?" and "What kind of help would be most useful to me?"

Summary of the Clearing Process

Becoming Present

Posture

> *Sit erect and balanced.

> *Relax your back.

> *Imagine a cord from the crown of your head suspending you from the ceiling.

Breathe like water

> *Breathe slowly and deeply.

> *Imagine air the consistency of water.

> *Inhale into deepest part of your abdomen first, and fill your lungs completely.

> *Use your stomach muscles to exhale.

> *Do three sets of four breaths.

Concentration

> *Listen to your inner silence.

Intending to clear

> *Question and test until the contraction is precisely located.

> *Ask: Am I ready to let go of this?

> *Respectfully request: Please do so now.

Setting the clearing

TAT

> *Place your thumb and middle finger on either side of the bridge of your nose.

> *Place your index finger in the center of your forehead just above the eyebrow line.

> *Hold until clear, not more than 90 sec.

> *Look for "release".

Cross-crawl

*Do a gentle march with a twist.

*Swing one knee high toward the other knee.

*Swing your arms to the opposite side in effect twisting your upper and lower body in different directions.

*Do this for 2-3 minutes.

Eye movement cross-crawl

*Close your eyes.

*Look alternately from your far left to your far right and back again.

*Repeat for 2 min or until a release is felt.

Chapter 14
Beyond Allergies

Psychonoetic testing is an incredible investigative and diagnostic tool. Despite what the medical profession would have you believe, most illnesses, major and minor, are not due to a deficiency of pharmaceutical drugs, but rather to something that you are doing, feeling, breathing, eating, or contacting. That is, they are related to lifestyle, emotional or physical stress, diet, or environment.

Whenever you have indigestion, a headache, a skin problem, or any of the other minor annoyances that your body presents, PsychoNoetics can help you locate the cause. I suggest using psychonoetic investigation in combination with other sorts of research, and of course, with the aid of other health practitioners. However, even licensed health practitioners are not always right in their diagnoses and prescriptions. Therefore, I use psychonoetic testing to double check the diagnoses of other practitioners. The combination is dynamite.

In general, when you are not feeling well, start with PsychoNoetics to find out what's wrong, clear memories, and keep asking questions to guide your further self-treatment. Once you start using the techniques, you will be surprised at the myriad ways you can adapt them to your own purposes and contexts.

Minor illnesses

By now, the understanding should be dawning that almost the entire operation of the body can be available to you through psychonoetic inquiry. Even more amazingly, the entire body is responsive to your instructions. The following example and protocol is useful for inquiries into other aspects of dis-ease beyond the case of allergies.

Remember to check and set your polarities by asking your training questions.

1. If you are feeling sick and suspect an illness, ask:
    Am I having an allergic reaction? (I always ask the question that I don't suspect first, to guard against a self-fulfilling answer.)
    No
    Am I getting sick?
    Yes

2. Once you determine that you're getting sick, you're on to the next stage of questioning, diagnosis. Ask:
    Is it an infection?
    Yes
    Is it a bacterial infection?
    No
    Is it a viral infection?
    No
    Is it serious or life threatening?
    No

Is it some variety of the common cold?
Yes

3. Once you have diagnosed the ailment, you can go on to ask
    questions about treatment:
    Would be in my best interests to go ice skating this afternoon
    if I feel better?
    No
    Will taking antibiotics help me get better faster?
    No
    Would be prudent to call in sick and stay in bed today?
    Yes
    Do I need the attention of a health care provider?
    No

Autoimmune disorders

In my psychonoetic investigations, despite the fact that my
specialty is the psyche, I have found myself again and again
venturing into the realm of physical disorders. Part of this has
been for my own sake, and part is because many times when a
client presents with a psychological issue, part of the problem
rests in the physical realm. The body/mind does not honor the
boundary that we "create" between our physical and mental
aspects. Allergies are one example where the boundary between
body and mind blurs. I have found that autoimmunity is
another.

In fact, an autoimmune disorder can be considered a special
case of an allergy, where someone becomes allergic to a part of
his or her own body. Just as allergic responses are attempts by
the immune system to reject an allergen, an autoimmune
disorder is the body's attempt to reject some part of itself.
Because of this, these types of illnesses can become very serious
indeed. In rheumatoid arthritis, the rejection affects the joints;
in multiple sclerosis the rejection attacks the nervous system.

Again, I am not an M.D., and I'm not giving you medical
advice. However, I believe that autoimmune disorders are on a

continuum with allergic and/or toxic reactions. In fact, many times they start with continual exposures to unrecognized allergies and/or toxins. PsychoNoetics can track down the connections and lay the groundwork for effective treatment plans.

For example, a client of mine came down with a form of rheumatoid arthritis, which then advanced into multiple chemical sensitivities. Upon investigation this history emerged. First, she came down with a strange flu-like sickness while working in an office which was being redecorated (in a building which was a closed environment). She stayed home for a week, recovered, went back to work and got sick again. She returned home again, stayed for a few weeks, then recovered, went back to work and started having crippling back pains, which were later diagnosed as a rare form of rheumatoid arthritis. Again, she went home to recover and never did.

Ten years later she consulted me for a very different problem, one of a psychological nature. Psychonoetic testing revealed that not only her psychological symptoms of mental fogginess, disorientation, and chronic anxiety, but also her arthritis were due to multiple chemical sensitivities, sensitivities that began when the office she worked in was redecorated. The chemicals, particularly the formaldehyde that was outgassing from the carpet adhesives had undermined her health to the point where she developed multiple chemical sensitivities.

After the course of psychonoetic therapy, identifying and releasing all of the allergic memories that she had accumulated through this and associated experiences, plus working with a naturopathic physician to reinforce her immune system, she was able to return to a normal life.

Another client had a similar story. She was a beautician, breathing in all sorts of chemicals day after day. After a while she developed multiple allergies and chemical sensitivities. When she first came to me, she had migraine headaches, joint and muscle pain, and periods of psychological disorientation. She had to stay indoors all day with the roar of an air filter as her constant companion. After a similar course of psychonoetic therapy, she regained her health and the joy of living.

Chronic illnesses

Like autoimmune disorders, many chronic illnesses also have their origin in repeated exposure to toxins and/or allergens. Again, psychonoetic investigations can be invaluable for tracking down the culprits. Take the example of common heartburn.

Millions of people suffer from heartburn, which is caused by the reflux of stomach acid into the esophagus. Antacids and acid blockers are a billion dollar business, and the drug companies seem to be using scare tactics to label common heartburn as *acid reflux disease* so that they can sell more pills.

Through psychonoetic testing and consulting kinesiological chiropractors, I have come to understand that drinking coffee, especially strong coffee, often irritates the valve called the cardiac sphincter. This valve, situated between the stomach and the esophagus, opens when we swallow food and then closes again so that the food and the digestive juices are contained in the stomach. When irritated, the inflammation keeps the valve from closing securely, and it lets stomach acid into the esophagus.

Another common irritant of the esophagus and cardiac sphincter can be carbonated beverages. Heavy intake of sodas and beer is linked to acid reflux disorder which is in turn linked to esophageal cancer. Testing on my fingers, I have gotten these connections time and time again, and many of my clients have found out that their digestive problems have cleared up completely by eliminating or at least curtailing their coffee intake and/or their intake of the fizzy stuff.

Hiatal hernia is a related problem in which the top of the stomach herniates or protrudes through the irritated and weak or opened valve. This is a painful condition that can mimic a heart attack and has sent many an unsuspecting sufferer to the emergency room. It also leads to serious complications. One of these is that the stomach is secreting its acids directly into the esophagus creating severe heartburn and maybe even an esophageal ulcer.

The body, responding to the hiatal hernia and not wanting to burn a hole in the esophagus, reduces its production of hydrochloric acid. This, in turn, severely disrupts the stomach's ability to digest protein, which leads to the leaky gut syndrome and protein toxicity. The chain of dis-ease continues as the pancreas tries to do the digestive task of the stomach acid, potentially leading to pancreatic insufficiency and even diabetic symptoms.

To bring the circle around completely, a food allergy in combination with heavy consumption of coffee or carbonated beverages, leads to abdominal bloating and an irritated cardiac sphincter and is a great recipe for cooking up the hiatal hernia in the first place.

Isn't it remarkable that all of the above information seems less available than the teachings of the secret mystery school of Ra, while drugs that conceal the symptoms without addressing the cause are hawked on prime-time television? It is clearly time to develop our own paths of inquiry, our own self-knowledge and evaluation to counter this trend, and psychonoetic protocols can do this for anyone willing to take the step toward self-authority.

Stress and adrenal exhaustion

Another common problem for us all is stress, both allergic and emotional, with its accompanying adrenal exhaustion. The adrenal glands become dysfunctional with chronic stress; they perceive our situation as one of persistent emergency and produce appropriate hormones until they can no longer do so.

When we reach adrenal exhaustion, we become lethargic, irritable and susceptible to all sorts of illnesses and psychological disturbances. Furthermore, when we are stressed out and our adrenals are exhausted, we tend to want coffee or other stimulants. These actually squeeze the last drops of juice out of our adrenal glands and make a bad problem worse.

Adrenal exhaustion from stress is a ubiquitous problem, one that weakens the body and leads to all sorts of complications. Again, with psychonoetic inquiry we can discover the root memories or responses, and upon discovery we can clear them.

The psychonoetic protocol for a physical problem

Allergies and related disorders above are examples of how complex the workings of our body are. However, with an investigative tool like PsychoNoetics we can unravel the story of any problem wherever it leads.

For example, problems with muscles, bones, and joints may stem from problems in usage like being overweight, misalignment, bad shoes, and repetitive strain like jogging or typing. But they may also be caused by allergies, toxic foods, and substances, and even glandular and organ imbalances which blow out the meridians through which the muscles receive energy. I have found that for any given person, the network of causation for their problems is a unique expression of their consciousness and lifestyle.

Until we integrate psychonoetic testing into our kit of wellness technologies, we will remain over-dependent on expensive and invasive testing technologies. Then, when we are diagnosed, we will tend to be subjected to the standard treatment for that diagnosis without taking into account our individuality. It is clearly time to reclaim our own lineage of experience, and to take responsibility for investigating the cause of our own dis-ease and releasing it!

Following is another example of a 20 Questions inquiry into a physical problem.

1. When you experience headache, abdominal bloating, and lethargy, ask:
   Do I know why I have recurrent bouts of headache, abdominal bloating and lethargy?

Yes
Is it a psychological or emotional problem?
No
Is it a physical problem?
Yes
Is the cause a disease state?
No
Is the cause an endocrine imbalance or insufficiency?
No
Is the cause environmental?
No
Is the cause an allergy?
No
Is the cause an ingestant?
Yes

2. Now the hunt for the specific ingestant and diagnosis begins. Ask:
Is it a medicine or supplement that I am taking?
No
Is it a beverage?
No
Is it a food?
Yes
Is the food dairy?
No
Is it a grain?
Yes
Is it corn?
No
Is it wheat?
Yes
Is it only wheat?
No
Is it all glutinous grains?
Yes

Am I gluten intolerant?
Yes

3. Having exposed the situation, continue to inquire for details, aiming for an appropriate response. Ask:
Is this an allergy that can be cleared permanently?
No
Is it in the best interests of my health to refrain from eating all glutinous grains entirely?
Yes
Can I eat wheat occasionally without ill effects?
Yes
How often can I eat wheat? (Now we ask a series of yes/no questions to arrive at an answer.)
Every day?
No
Every two days?
No
Every three days?
No
Every four days?
Yes
Am I currently having an allergic reaction to wheat?
Yes

4. Proceed to clear the present reaction. Ask:
Am I ready to clear that reaction?
Yes
Please do so now!

5. Potentiate the clearing with TAT or cross-crawl. Then ask:
Is my allergic reaction cleared?
Yes

As you can see, the 20 questions technique identifies the causes of a problem in stages. First, a general diagnosis is sought, here, for example, a problem with an ingestant is found. Then, a specific diagnosis zeroed in on, here, the problem of gluten intolerance. Next, a course of action is confirmed, and finally, if there's something to clear, a clearing is done.

It may be that to completely release a particular configuration of ill health, many more inquiries must be made, and some assistance sought. However, compared to the typical medical experience, this avenue of self-discovery and empowerment leaves no scars, and enhances rather than dissipates our capacity for self-healing.

Testing drugs, supplements, and other remedies

You can further use psychonoetic inquiry to identify specific remedies and even evaluate foods, supplements, and drugs. For instance, you can determine whether a specific herb or vitamin will assist with a health problem that you are having. For example...

1. To evaluate whether something will strengthen your fingernails, ask:
   Is there a supplement that will strengthen my nails?
   Yes
   Is it a vitamin?
   No
   Is it an herb?
   No
   Is it a foodstuff?
   No
   Is it a mineral?
   Yes
   Is it calcium?
   Yes
   Is it a particular form of calcium?
   Yes

2. When you have established that it is a particular form of calcium, you could go to your local natural foods store, assemble all the different kinds of available calcium supplements and test them. First, take three or four in your hands, so that your body has a chance to register their energy relative to one another. Then, pick up each in turn and ask:
    Of the three (or four) forms of calcium here, is this best for my nails?
    Repeat the question three or four times until you receive a yes *answer.*

3. Take the winner, and hold it in your hands with another two or three samples. Then, repeat the process. Do this until you have selected the best supplement for your body.

If you have a open-minded physician, you can also evaluate pharmaceuticals in this way, trying out multiple drugs until you find one that will suit you. The technique can also be used to address a drug's side effects. If you don't have an open-minded physician, try to find one!

1. To explore whether a problem is a side effect of a drug, ask:
    Do you know what is giving me hives?
    Yes
    Is it something I am eating?
    No
    Is it emotional?
    No
    Is it a drug I am taking?
    Yes
    Is it penicillin?
    Yes
    Am I allergic to penicillin?
    Yes
    Can this allergy be cleared?
    Yes

2. Proceed to clear the allergy.
   Are you ready to clear this allergy?
   Yes
   Please clear it now.

3. Set the clearing with TAT or cross-crawl. Ask:
   Is in my best interests to keep on taking penicillin?
   No
   Should I experiment with another antibiotic?
   Yes

Be informed as well as open to intuition

You can see clearly that my questioning is both informed and intuitive. Using these techniques is no excuse for not being as well informed as possible about the problem you're dealing with. The more information, the better the questions you can create to focus clearly into the heart of the matter at hand.

With practice PsychoNoetics becomes a window into your intuition as well. Questions seem to arise that are the right questions and soon the journey of self-discovery becomes easier and less random.

I believe that this marriage of traditional information and self-discovery is a powerful foreshadowing of how we will move ahead in consciousness toward self-care that is easy, graceful, and *rapid*! Again, if you know an open-minded health practitioner, the collaboration of reason and intuition will be greatly facilitated by working together as you practice PsychoNoetics.

Chapter 15
Clearing the Mind

Every time we start to feel sick with symptoms - like a cold, an upset stomach, intestinal bloating, a rash, or unexplained sleepiness, we can suspect an allergy or an illness and check for it. If we isolate a difficulty through testing, we know that it's time to clear.

But *how do we know when we are in the grips of a psychological memory* with its accompanying perceptual misinterpretations and distortions? Most of us experience our inner self as one seamless interaction with our world; we go from one thing to another never noticing the moments of change when our state of being moves from contented to upset. How do we begin to even *suspect* ourselves of being in memory?

Becoming our own internal sleuth
There are two answers to the question of how to notice when we are in psychological memory: a little answer and a bigger one. The little one is about social adjustment and absence of

pain. It is what we go to psychotherapists for. The big one is about really being in reality. It is about radical sanity, awakening, and enlightenment. It is what we do meditation and go to spiritual teachers for.

Let's start with the little answer. Whenever we are in the grips of an uncomfortable emotion, whenever we are feeling anything that we don't want to feel, whenever we are feeling emotional pain or discomfort, we should check to see whether we are in memory - because nine times out of ten, we will be! *Any negative emotion, fear, anger, hatred, aversion,* lets us know that there's something to let go of. Likewise, *any negative energy state like depression, boredom, or anxiety* is also a signal to check ourselves out.

The bigger answer, the one that opens the door to spiritual evolution, is that whenever we are in the grips of any emotion at all, positive or negative, particularly one *that propels us to action* we should check to see whether we are in memory!

Positive feelings and aroused states, although we do not experience them as problems, can just as easily be signs that we are in the grips of a memory. Feelings of superiority, invulnerability, self-righteousness, and being chosen, as well as aroused states like elation, righteous anger, spiritual or religious ecstasy, and being messianic, to name a few, can be the flip side, the ego compensation for negative feelings and self-rejection. At the very least, they should give us occasion to pause and investigate.

These *up* feelings and states, are potentially negative in the sense of being *unbalanced* - and therefore they can be destructive to ourselves and others. Consider, for example, how overprotective mothers and over-disciplinary fathers can destroy children's lives while trying to protect them. More extreme examples are overzealous missionaries that destroy indigenous cultures while trying to bring the natives to Jesus, and even suicide bombers that consciously destroy themselves and others for what they believe to be a holy cause.

Many of these people are well intentioned, selfless and even self-sacrificing, full of righteousness, and full of the conviction that they are doing the right thing. They don't even suspect that they may be delusional, dangerous and destructive! Aroused, compensatory feelings and states can be more dangerous than depressed self-rejecting ones, because they feel so good that they are not suspected for what they are - and because they so often lead to extreme and unwise acts.

Monitoring

Clearing practice begins with *monitoring;* staying mindful of your state of consciousness or degree of presence, so that you don't slip into a contracted, depressed, defensive, or agitated state, or its opposite, over-arousal, mania, or euphoria. When you feel yourself slipping into either of these extreme states of consciousness, it is the time to investigate whether you have anything to clear.

Paradoxically, however, we can only be mindful from mindfulness, from the right place. We can't see without a place from which to see. When we are in the right place, monitoring and clearing can help us preserve it. But we first have to be in the right place, and if we are not there, we have to get there. Most of spiritual development is just about getting into this right place and staying there.

So we have to get into this right place—but what is it and what does it feel like? Most of us are not clear on it, nor do we commonly get much help in the matter. We are in a culture that does not value the right place; indeed, for the most part, it does not even recognize it! They say that the Inuit people have over 60 words for snow while we just have one. But at least we have one. Although there is a minority growing aware of a place of inner rightness, the mainstream of Western culture does not even have one word for *the right place.* The words it uses, words like sane, well-adjusted, religious, even spiritual and loving, are so biased by unexamined cultural beliefs that they do not convey the quality of *right place* at all.

Presence

So what is this *right place*? First of all, it is not emotional, at least not in the way we commonly think of emotions. Most of what we experience as emotions is really a call to defensive action, or - in the case of some negative emotions like fear - inhibition. Even that most exalted of emotions, love, can be the justification for possessiveness, clinging, jealousy, control, competitiveness, and a score of other reactions.

What we want is to be in a place that is calm and clear, but full of feeling. We want to feel alive, but at peace, satisfied and connected, in harmony with the world, not having to do anything, but with the sense that we are able to do everything. We want to feel centered in the here and now. This is the right place, and my favorite word for it is **presence**. We want to be in presence. We want to be present. If we learn what it feels like when we are centered in the here and now, when we are in *presence*, then any deviation from the right place will be readily apparent and will be our sign that it is time for a clearing!

When was the last time you were really present? Unless you are very unfortunate, unless you are one of those tortured souls who never lets themselves rest, you have had numerous experiences of presence.

People touch presence in all sorts of ways, looking at a sunset, talking with an old friend, holding their sleeping child, singing in the shower, making love. Presence is in some sense the psychological analogy of perfect health. Presence is coming to rest in a place where you're all right and the world is all right, where there is nothing to do but be present. Presence is a state in which you are in total acceptance of all aspects of your being.

We all strive for presence, but we are not always aware of what we are doing. When we make ourselves a drink or smoke a cigarette or a joint, when we turn on soothing music, when we take a walk or swim, *when we do anything, not for what it gets us, but for how much it makes us feel like ourselves, we are seeking presence.* When we seek love or sex sometimes what we are really seeking is presence. When we play with our children, not out of duty but out of impulse, when we pet a cat or smell a flower, we remember that that is the way we once experienced presence, and we are seeking it once again.

So think about it. When have you been in presence? What are the times when you were feeling completely all right with yourself, completely at home in the world? What did it feel like? These times, these feelings are the *right place*. This is where you should want to be all of the time. Any deviation, up or down, is suspect. You should take any deviation from presence as a falling out from grace; use it as an occasion to check for memories and, when you find them, to clear!

The difference between emotions and states of being

We live in a culture that idolizes emotion and distrusts presence. Every individual and every institution seems to be trying to control every other one by instilling the desired emotions in them. Whether they are advertisers trying to get you to buy their products, parents trying to get you to cut your hair, schools trying to get you to do your homework, recruiters trying to get you to join the Army, fundraisers trying to get you to support their cause or religious leaders trying to get you to believe and to lead what they think is a righteous life - they are all trying to control you by instilling emotions in you. Instead of uncovering this trick and even more, suspecting emotion itself, we allow ourselves to get hooked on emotions, to value them, even to seek them out. We look for the unbalanced and sometimes even desperate emotion of "romantic love" as a confirmation of suitability when choosing a mate. We are drawn to emotional people, (as long as they are not depressed) and see them as having a great "personality", as deep people, even as charismatic leaders. Furthermore, we separate emotions into good ones and bad ones, oblivious of the fact that we are really making unexamined, value judgments and setting unexamined priorities.

Instead of seeking them out, we should be looking at emotions, all emotions, with suspicion, because all emotions have the quality of propelling us to take unexamined actions, and these actions are usually, if not always, *reactions*. Furthermore, having a reaction invariably indicates that we are in some sort of memory, and that it is time to investigate and perhaps clear.

Awakening and enlightenment are all about getting *unemotional* and becoming present. However, getting unemotional and becoming present *does not mean becoming unfeeling*. Rather it brings about *states of being* that are much more deeply felt and enlivening than emotional reactions. Peace, unconditional love, compassion, awareness, humor, curiosity, aliveness, alertness and the like are all states of being, or perhaps flavors of that *one* state of being which is *presence*.

Getting present

So it is time move away from emotional reactions and cultivate presence in their place. You can use the preparation techniques from the preceding chapters for getting present or you may already have your own.

Many forms of meditation, prayer, Tai Chi Chuan, yoga and the like, when done mindfully, will get you present. Other things that have the potential to get you present are taking a long walk, looking at the ocean, playing with a child or a pet, jogging, or even taking a hot bath. Find out what works for you. What is important is that you know what it feels like when you are in presence.

For the sake of this discussion let's talk about three states of consciousness: present, not quite present (not there, but close enough so that you know you're not there), and clueless.

Present

When we're present, all problems disappear, and monitoring what is happening becomes natural. From presence, when something pulls you off center (into *not quite present*), it is immediately apparent and available for clearing.

There is a long-standing tradition in the east of becoming present by meditating, doing yoga, chanting mantras. This might appeal to our spiritual side and is good training, but it is hard to do when you're teaching a class or taking care of your kids.

In addition, in order to stay present, most of us have the tendency to avoid people and situations that are disturbing. This is usually a mistake. Avoiding the occasions when your issues arise is not going to furnish you with grist for the clearing mill. Allowing oneself to move from presence into the tension of *not quite present* and back again is actually more useful for following the clearing path.

Not quite present

Most of us who are advanced on a spiritual path alternate between being present and not quite. It is important to know that being *not quite present* is not a problem; it has the advantage of enough presence available to see an arising area of difficulty. As you get caught in memories and become not quite present, the formerly unconscious difficulties held by the egoic self become visible, i.e., you become more conscious to yourself. It is from this double weighted consciousness, when the problem is apparent, that clearing is possible.

Monitoring yourself is easiest when you're fully present because losing presence by contrast is very dramatic and apparent. However, when you're *not quite present*, so long as you are aware of it and can manage the tension, your awareness of a problem is more detailed because the problem occupies a greater percentage of your inner space. What needs to be cleared can be focused very precisely from the *not quite present* space.

Because of the inherent tension in being not quite present, there is some danger of losing presence altogether, forgetting what presence feels like, and thinking that you're there when you're not. But there's no shame or blame in losing presence; we learn from every moment's experience. Next time you'll be more aware.

In the meantime, learning what it feels like to move out of presence altogether, to be able to admit that we are not present, is a great achievement. From this learning we are able to monitor ourselves, even when we "lose it". This is staying open to growth at all times, even when we're not in presence.

Cluelessness

Cluelessness, however, presents a real problem. When we are not present and completely unaware of the fact, there is no motivation to change and that presents a very difficult situation. Self-confident cluelessness is even more refractory because underlying it is denial, denial of the pain, aridity, and self-loathing that is the constant companion of non-presence.

All of the really dangerous people in the world, dangerous both to themselves and others, are simultaneously clueless, over-confident, and self-inflated. These are the people who hold doggedly to their accomplishments, identities, opinions, affiliations, etc., never examining the impact of their behaviors, right or wrong, constructive or destructive, for better or for worse. These are the people who believe that what they think makes them right, and that everyone who doesn't agree with them is wrong!

In order to be open to change, you have first to be open to yourself, to the possibility that you are not perfect, and to the acceptance of that imperfection.

The psychonoetic protocol for clearing memories

OK, so you are monitoring and you feel the negative emotions pulling you from presence. Or you just know that you're not present because you remember the times you have been, and they didn't feel like this. Now what do you do?

1. If you are a newcomer to PsychoNoetics, review Chapters 8-12 to refresh your memory. Ask your training questions to be sure your polarity is established correctly.

2. Test yourself to answer the following questions. Use your favorite way of testing, either the O-ring finger test, the pendulum, or any of the ways you feel comfortable with, to receive *yes* or *no* answers. Ask yourself, either out loud or sub-vocally:
   Am I in memory? (Or are you perceiving from remembered conclusions?)
   Yes
   Do I know when these memories originated?
   Yes
   Do I know what these memories are?
   Yes
   Am I ready to clear these memories?
   Yes

3. Use your presencing techniques (above and Chapter 9) to come back to presence, so that the clearing will be optimally effective as a request from our highest Selves.

(When testing for allergies, we do preparation exercises before we start, to presence ourselves. However, in psychological clearings, when we do not know precisely what is going on, but suspect we are in memory, we do not want to move deeply into presence and out of memory because we will lose our awareness of the problem. When we are in memory, our unconscious mind knows what memories it is holding and can focus precisely on what needs to be cleared. When we move completely out of memory and into presence, our unconscious mind doesn't identify precisely what it is we are asking to be cleared. We invite our highest most coherent presence only after we have isolated the contraction...as we begin to clear.

4. Do the clearing as a gentle and loving request from yourself to yourself. Say:
    Please clear these memories now.

5. Set the clearing with TAT, the thinker, cross-crawl, or eye movement cross-crawl (Chapter 12). Observe your feelings again and see if they have lightened up. If they have done so, the clearing has been successful.

What to do if you are not ready to clear

Sometimes we test *no*, we are *not ready* to clear a memory. Looking closely, we may even feel our whole body resisting the change. In these cases usually the problem is an associated memory that must be cleared first, in order for the problem at hand to be released.

1. When we obtain a *no* answer for the question, "Am I ready to clear these memories?" ask:
    Is this memory pinned by earlier memories?
    Yes
    Do I know when these earlier memories have originated?
    Yes
    Do I know what these memories are?
    Yes
    Am I ready to clear these memories?
    Yes

2. Presence yourself as much as possible and clear. Say:
    Please do so now.

3. Set the clearing with TAT, the thinker, cross-crawl, or eye movement cross-crawl. Most of the time, this secondary clearing will unblock the primary memories, so they can be cleared.

4. Return to the original memory and ask:
   Am I now ready to clear the first memories?
   Yes

5. Presence yourself and lovingly say:
   Please do so now.

6. Set the clearing. Be aware of your body and inner space. Often, a palpable relaxation and lightness accompanies a successful clearing.

Very resistant memories

Sometimes the clearing still doesn't happen, because that which is pinning the memory is not a memory, but something like an attachment or a belief system. There are many nuances to our inner realities that are beyond the scope of this book, but there is a general follow up that can help.

1. If you still test *no* for the question "Are you ready to clear?", or are unable to clear, repeat the procedure leaving open what it is that is pinning the memory:
   Is there something else that is pinning this memory and resisting the clearing?
   Yes
   Do you know what it is?
   Yes
   Am I ready, willing and able to clear it?
   Yes

2. Do the clearing. Say:
   Please do so now.

3. Set the clearing.

4. Return to the original memories and ask again:
   Am I now ready to clear the first memories?
   Yes

5. Clear and set the clearing.

In doing these clearings you are the explorer and master of your own inner space. As you clear, you will discover your own subtleties on this technique. Some other words (besides memories) that I use regularly to focus consciousness on what needs to be cleared are: beliefs, identities, attachments, self-denials, judgments, blames, intentional distortions, emotions. They may be of use to you as well as you clear. Please contact me with any questions that arise as you liberate yourself from your own associations of memories and beliefs.

Clearing habits, addictions, and phobias
Habits, addictions, phobias, and all manner of neurotic symptoms that have an obsessive, compulsive, or involuntary nature share a similar origin. They are all avoidance strategies. They are basically strategies to avoid facing something, some deep feelings, some risky activity, or some feared outcome.

However, in almost every case these fears are exaggerated by a being in memory. This "memory"misinterprets and wildly exaggerates what is at worst a moderate risk to one's real well being. (There may, however, be a major risk to one's cherished ideas of themselves.) Often releasing these remembered conclusions begins the unraveling of associative learning that holds the problem in place.

1. When in the grip of the compulsion, inquire whether you are in memory. If you get a confirmation, you can proceed to clear it like any other memory. Follow the above procedure.

2. After clearing memories, proceed to clear the symptoms themselves. If you test *yes* that you can let go of the

symptoms, proceed to clear and set the clearing. If not, investigate further. For example:

Can I let go of my compulsive eating?

No

Is this clearing blocked by a secondary gain, something I am avoiding?

Yes

Do you know what this is?

Yes

3. Let your intuition guide your investigation. Open yourself to insight, see what questions come to you, ask them, and then test the answers:

Am I avoiding a feeling?

No

Am I avoiding a realization?

No

Am I avoiding doing something?

No

Am I avoiding a facet of my life?

Yes

Do you know what this facet of my life is?

Yes

Is a work-related?

No

Is it intimacy related?

Yes

Is it a romantic relationship?

Yes

Am I avoiding romantic involvements?

Yes

Is it because I fear being hurt?

Yes

4. At some point you will come to the heart of the issue. It may take a few rounds of investigation, but when you hit the

mark, usually you feel something ring true. When you feel complete, it is time to ask about memories and try clearing the symptoms again. Ask:
When I fear being hurt, am I in memory?
Yes
Do I know what these memories are?
Yes
Am I ready to clear these memories?
Yes

5. Clear the memories, check whether you can release the compulsion now, clear that, and set the clearings:
Please do so now.
Am I ready now to let go of compulsive eating?
Yes
Please do so now.

Review of protocol

If you have been reading and practicing the protocols, you should be developing an instinct on how to clear by now. First, you ask whether or not you are in memory. Then, you test to get an answer. If you get a confirmation, you ask whether your unconscious knows these memories. Then, if you get a confirmation on this, ask whether you are ready to clear. Then, of course, you clear and set the clearing.

If you don't get a confirmation, use 20 Questions to investigate further, pursuing the problem until you get a confirmation that you're ready to clear. After clearing, ask if there is something else that you need to let go of. If there is, just adapt the process as in the above example.

I have not given you precise protocols for clearing every possible problem of body and mind. However, used with the book's message as a whole, the examples I *have* given you, are an entry point to a path of greater self-awareness and self-authority.

Importantly, the protocol rests in a conceptual framework, a way of understanding that all kinds of physical and emotional dysfunctions originate in remembered conclusions *that are clearable.* We are confirmed that there is a way to release the seemingly intractable baggage that we have carried around for so long. We now have a tool for identifying and unlearning whatever has ceased to be applicable in the present and instead has become problematic and dysfunctional.

But in order to make optimum use of the tools of PsychoNoetics, you have to use then consciously. 1) Study what is known and written about the problem you are experiencing, whether it is physiological or psychological. If nothing else, the information you bring will furnish you with the questions to ask. 2) Apply logic. Twenty Questions is an analytic game. The testing is automatic, but knowing what questions to ask and in what order takes thought. 3) Trust intuitive knowing. Open yourself to receiving insight and inspiration from a source beyond your known self. Because of the testing process, you have a check against going astray which makes opening yourself to intuition almost entirely safe.

If you try to use this book as a cookbook, looking to it to answer your every question and guide you every step of the way, you'll be disappointed and frustrated. However, if you look to it to provide you with understandings and tools to use in your own self-empowerment, you'll find it invaluable and you'll soon master the technique, making it your own and finding numerous ways to apply it to your own life. This protocol is only the beginning. The rest remains up to you.

Chapter 16
Following the Clearing Path

Feelings and thoughts cannot be cleared unless they are accepted. In fact, the clearing implies the acceptance.

What do we let go to?

When we let go, what do we let go to? This is a question I have been posing for almost 10 years and, as my understanding has advanced, I have reformulated the answer almost as many times. When we are using PsychoNoetics for psychotherapeutic purposes, letting go of a memory or belief, we just let go of that, and we let go *to whatever is left*. That which is left is our ordinary self minus the problem we have just released.

But PsychoNoetics may also be used as a path to Self-realization, what I call "The Clearing Path". The use of PsychoNoetics as a *sacred technology* is in one sense, no different than the therapeutic use. That is, we are always letting go *to whatever is left*. Yet, there is a difference in how we approach the practice of letting go, in what we intend to accomplish. Our intention in letting go may be problem-solving, or it may be a different kind of intention, a *sacred intention*.

The sacred intention is to let go all the way, awaken to our true nature, and become enlightened. This entails not only disidentifying from one's ego, but also deconstructing it. (The great mistake of the new age, one that undermines many spiritual pursuits, is that the pursuit of enlightenment is often used to enhance one's ego rather than to deconstruct it. If some of the people pursuing spiritual paths realized that they were signing up for ego annihilation rather than ego enhancement, they would be horrified.)

When we let go on the Clearing Path, instead of intending to let go to our egoic identity (as we customarily feel it and hold it), we intend to let go to our highest level of spiritual realization. This highest realization is that our real identity is the state of presence, the intrinsic perfection of pure consciousness, and *still mind* is the portal to it. The practice of letting go becomes a powerful route to *still mind*, potentiating and synergizing with any other spiritual paths that we may walk.

So, on the "clearing path", we intend to let go, not to our customary self, but *all the way*. This is the sacred intention, and when we align with it, each clearing becomes a steppingstone to enlightenment.

The therapeutic intention and the sacred intention

What is the difference, if any, between the ordinary use of PsychoNoetics as a therapeutic or healing technique and using PsychoNoetics as a spiritual path? Let's explore the difference in intention.

The therapeutic intention is not to lose one's ego or transform oneself. It is to become less conflicted and more successful while continuing to do exactly what we are doing. Of course, we are willing to shift a bit in order to make things better, but as little as possible. (This is similar to the philosophy of allopathic medicine, where the emphasis is on alleviating symptoms rather than diagnosing the cause of the disease and changing the lifestyle, which nine times out of ten is the cause.)

When we are on the Clearing Path, our intention is nothing short of self-transformation and ultimately, enlightenment. This is the sacred intention. We understand that the cause of our conflict is the set of ideas that we hold about ourselves, we are willing to let them go, and we jump into the river of change toward complete realization of who we are.

It is important to examine our intentions in life. The life-intentions of egoic, mind-identified people are generally about survival, success, acquisition, and power. The life-intentions of awakening people are more about authenticity, clarity, peace, and making things better.

A hypothetical example will make this point clearer. Let us say that a woman is interested in getting someone to marry her. With the help of her friends, she maps out a campaign to get him to propose. However, she has some "psychological"issues that thwart her plans. One of these is that whenever she is with someone she wants to impress, she gets self-conscious and tongue-tied. Clearing with a psychotherapeutic intention, she identifies a cluster of memories that support the conclusion that she is an inconsequential person and nothing that she says is important or memorable. She successfully clears those memories and as a result, finds it much easier to talk spontaneously. However, her intention was *not* to realize her true identity, not to clear all the way. It was only to remove some obstacles to her plans. Clearing those memories, she becomes better able to pursue her campaign of seduction.

However, there is more, much more for this woman to see. The whole notion of waging a campaign of seduction in order to get someone to marry her, implies a negative, self image and virtually guarantees that she is not going to present herself authentically in other ways. This almost assures that even if she succeeds in marrying, the marriage is going to get into trouble as hidden aspects of her personality emerge.

The sacred intention, on the other hand, would be to let go completely - all the way to an empty still mind, with the understanding that one's real nature would assert itself from that place. Then, our hypothetical woman would be free to pursue an authentic relationship, with complete openness about her aims, needs, and even shortcomings. This is more than letting go to still mind; it is letting go with the understanding that still mind is the portal to enlightenment and the gateway to heaven on earth.

How does sacred intention change the clearing?

Whenever you do a psychonoetic clearing, your psyche spontaneously restructures itself around the new, inner reality. In the therapeutic use of PsychoNoetics, when you let go to what is left (whatever you're holding that you are not ready to let go of), your psyche spontaneously restructures itself around what you are still holding.

So, for instance, in the above example, the woman is still left with the intention to seduce and with a self-concept of unlovability. However, if she had intended to let go all the way, not only of her difficulties, but also of the need and intention to seduce, her clearing and the subsequent restructuring of her psyche would be much more radical.

Before I understood this, I was mystified by the fact that for some people clearing was almost earth-shaking, while for others the effect was unremarkable, sometimes almost indiscernible. Finally, it dawned on me that people could only clear as far as they intended to. If they intended to hold onto their ordinary self they would, and there was not much I could do about it. (This, by the way is part of the reason why the PsychoNoetics is not an ordinary, self-help modality, but has to be presented in an authentic, spiritual context.)

Qualities of mind

In following the Clearing Path, four qualities of mind are especially important. The first is the ability to be present, to go into your inner silence or emptiness and function from it. The second is a modicum of understanding. If you are wedded to naïve perception, the worldview of separate things ruled by the Newtonian laws of nature, you will have difficulty accepting PsychoNoetics. The third is trust. You have to have faith in yourself and the power of your intention, the power of consciousness, the power of what you are. Then, and only then, will you be able to suspend the illusion of separation, give up on trying to make things happen from mind, and access that vast field of consciousness, the psychonoetic field, that you are in - and that is in you.

The fourth and perhaps the most important quality of mind is acceptance. Feelings and thoughts cannot be cleared until they are accepted. In fact, the clearing implies the acceptance. Before you can let go of something, be it memory, thought, or feeling, you have to accept that you're holding it...and that it's OK, that it doesn't make you a terrible person.

Now this is an almost self-evident psychological principle, one that needs no research to prove it. You will have trouble accepting your shortcomings in direct proportion to your need to reject them. If you are so self-critical that you have a hard time accepting criticism, even constructive criticism, if you're so insecure that even a suggestion that something about yourself is not perfect sends you into a tizzy, you will have a hard time changing.

Because they are based upon self-testing, the techniques of PsychoNoetics facilitate acceptance. Self-testing cannot be construed as criticism or attack, and even highly self-judgmental people can use them. Yet, there is always a danger that some people will reject self-testing whole cloth, because of their resistance to any idea that they are not as perfect as they feel the need to be.

Accepting the fear that something is wrong with us
All of us, even the most secure, have some degree of defensiveness (because we identify our ideas about ourselves

with our physical body, see Chapter 6). When we hold inferiority feelings, insecurities, and self-doubts, we are compelled to defend or compensate for them by being superior, if not perfect. Commonly, these feelings lead us to deny any and all personality flaws and to aggressively assert our emotions, opinions, and rights.

Denialism

You can see this psychodynamic seesaw of inferiority and superiority, denial and aggression, at work not only in yourself and other individuals, but also in collectives. You see it in minority movements like gay rights, militant feminism, and black power - and even in fundamentalist sects. Wherever we find a person or a people with strong inferiority feelings, we find this combination of denial and aggression. For linguistic convenience, let's call this the denial syndrome or denialism.

Denialism in individuals is by far the most common source of psychological problems and the greatest obstacle to personal and spiritual growth! Everything from hysteria to personality disorders to uncontrollable rage and prejudice can be traced back to denialism. Beyond that, collective denialism destroys corporations, economies, cultures, and even nations. Denialism keeps people and peoples from facing reality. It is axiomatic that there is no problem that can be solved by denying reality, and no problem that cannot be solved by facing it.

Recognition and acceptance

Recognizing this denial, and the underlying fear that something is wrong with us, may be the first step we need to take on the Clearing Path. We cannot change if we are standing in our own way, denying that there is anything we want to change.

So the first thing that we need to do on the clearing path is accept - accept that we are not lacking, broken, or in any way inferior to anybody else; we are just conditioned differently - accept the unworthy feelings and thoughts that we identify through introspection and testing; they are just mistaken conclusions.

On the level of our real identity we are perfect, and we share that perfection with all sentient beings. Any imperfections we have are on the level of our bodies, our histories, our finances, or our existential situation. Asserting our intrinsic perfection is not denialism; denial of this intrinsic perfection is.

The doctrine of original sin, (meaning badness) is perhaps the greatest sin (meaning a wrong turn) of all time. Any doctrine that teaches people that they are intrinsically bad, defective, inferior, imperfect or devoid of God nature, is either a grievous mistake or a calculated ploy, meant to control and enslave them. This condemnation, applies equally to parents, schools, religious institutions, corporations, cultures, governments, and all others that would go down that path. The teaching and embrace of the doctrine that human kind is basically imperfect or evil, have led to nothing but folly. (This does not mean that we don't have anything to learn, or that we don't need to grow. It is just that, paradoxically, we have to grow toward accepting our inherent divinity, and these doctrines stand firmly in the way of that.)

So I repeat, the first thing that we need to do on the clearing Path is accept our intrinsic perfection; this will allow us to accept our shortcomings and work on them. The journey begins and ends with the Self.

Chapter 17
Retroperceptions

Memories as held ideas, or conclusions about ourselves

I have already developed the idea that memories are actually conclusions that we have reached about a relationship between our world and ourselves. Because we use these memories as a matrix in which to interpret our present *perceptions*, I have given them the technical name of *retroperceptions, i.e.,* perceptions that go back to the past.

The process of retroperception is in many ways a normal process. It is how we incorporate our experiences into a coherent body of conclusions to which we may instantly refer whenever necessary. It is how children "learn" that fire hurts, so that the next time fire is encountered, it is "perceived" as a source of pain.

However, many of the conclusions we have come to in the past, especially in the psychological and social arenas, are false and counterproductive. For brevity's sake, let's call these

conclusions *maladaptive memories.* When such retroperceptions, untrue at the time or no longer true, are embedded in our
inner "body of conclusions", they foster further maladaptive
learning, and in fact, get us into a lot of trouble. Maladaptive
memories or retroperceptions need to be cleared or *unlearned*
for our perceptions and responses to be true and appropriate.

How retroperceptions create negative emotions

Let's further define and explore the concept of
retroperception.

*Retroperception Defn: 1. Retroactive perception. 2. The perception of
present events in the context of past experiences, thus re-attributing the
significance and re-experiencing the emotions that were present in the past.*

Our minds are associative. That's how we and all other
complex animals learn. Since we came into this world, we have
been learning by associating our experiences into categories.
These categories, then, become the context for the next thing
that is learned. They furnish a matrix into which to fit our
ongoing experiences and by which to interpret them.
Furthermore, every time we perceive something in the present,
two things happen. One, we re-experience the emotions that
were present when that category of experience was first
established. Two, we add the present event to the evolving
category of experience, thus further extending its coverage. This
process is the essence of *retroperception.*

Most retroperceptions originated in childhood and are
constantly bringing childhood feelings into the present for us to
relive them. Almost all childhood experiences, whatever
positive qualities they contain, also contain elements of
helplessness, vulnerability, and fear (that is the reality of most
childhoods). Traumatic memories contain the additional
qualities of terror and being overwhelmed. Most maladaptive
retroperceptions bring back the helplessness and vulnerability
of childhood. That is why they upset us emotionally, and that's

why letting go of them can return us to clarity, power, and above all, the emotional balance of our real identity.

Strategies for change

Since Freud, psychology has recognized the importance of retroperceptions, particularly maladaptive retroperceptions, although they have usually been referred to as repressed and/or unconscious traumatic memories. Up until the present time, psychotherapy has been mainly about retrieving these memories. The idea was that if you could only get in touch with them, it would give you insight into the source of your problems, and this insight, in turn, would make them go away. However, the indifferent success of psychotherapy in general testifies to the inadequacy of that paradigm. Getting in touch with memories is an important first step, but it isn't enough!

Following the lead of Wilhelm Reich, some psychotherapists have gone further. They have discovered that memories seem to hold energy and have devised ways to release this energy. Energy release is very dramatic. It is accompanied by emotional pyrotechnics, crying, laughing, screaming, and even violent shaking. Furthermore, it is accompanied in the short-term by a profound sense of relief, which in itself is very reinforcing and convinces the client that a momentous change has taken place.

However, despite the dramatic value of energy release, it, too, has proved disappointing in the long-term and is of questionable value as a therapeutic strategy. The theory was that if the energy of the memory was drained off, the trauma would be discharged. However, it did not work that way in practice. Instead, like Sinbad's cup which was connected to the sea, the supply of traumatic energy turned out to inexhaustible, and clients, once they developed the knack of discharging, began going off at the slightest provocation and at inappropriate times, thus making their social adjustment not better, but worse. (This problem got very acute in followers of the Primal Therapy of Janov.)

The reason for this is that memories are not really composed of emotional energy. Rather, they are just ideas, self-reflective thought forms. They interpret our perceptions and put the personal meaning into our experiences. It is meaning, personal meaning, that channels our store of emotional energy.

Therefore, in order to stop generating negative emotional energy, which is what we have to do in order to stop past traumas from reoccurring, we have to cut the negative emotional energy at its source. *We have to clear the maladaptive retroperceptions themselves.*

Chapter 18
The Suffering We Create

We have seen in previous chapters that we humans learn to construct ourselves and our world through retroperceptions. The advantage of this is that it enables us to instantly and automatically apply what we have learned in the past to our present situation. However, the disadvantage is that it locks us into perceptions that may not be true.

A more insidious disadvantage is that we are usually not aware that this is happening. Retroperception is invisible and imperceptible. When retroperceptions signal danger, often the only thing we are aware of is being emotionally hijacked, plunged into unexpected, inexplicable, and uncontrollable reactivity. These emotional hijackings, distressing as they are, can provide invaluable windows into our unconscious if we learn how to use them that way.

The unconscious arising

Those of us who are trying to lead aware, examined lives and to be good, loving people, know how hard it is to sustain this intention when we are stressed out or feel under attack. Despite our best efforts, our emotions derail us. When we are calm and relaxed, we have things under control, but then something happens. We inexplicably lose control and suddenly we become angry, depressed, resentful, fearful, or the like.

Usually, we feel that the source of our fear and pain is *out there*, the fault of other people or circumstances. Sometimes, we also realize that what is happening to us does not *fully justify* the stress we feel and how it makes us act, but yet we seem to be unable to do anything about it.

When negative emotions overtake us and we act badly, we feel regretful and demoralized. But most of all, we feel betrayed, betrayed by our emotions. Defensiveness comes over us inexplicably and without warning. Often, we don't know where it comes from; even if we do, we can't seem to do anything about it. About the most we can do is control our actions so that we don't show our emotions or let them force us to do anything we regret. But self-control is not the same as feeling relaxed and resting in love, not nearly.

When negative emotions overtake us, it is as if another part of us, a part that we know is there, but that we don't own as ourselves, comes between our best intentions and us. It is as if there is an entity within, almost an *enemy within*, which is taking control. Freud called this "entity within", the *unconscious* and alluded to it as a place in the mind.

But what is this unconscious and what role does it play in creating our suffering? One way that we could think about it is as an enormous, multi layered, instruction manual. And what does it contain instructions for?—*for survival.* These survival instructions reside on every level of the largely unconscious system that is you: genetic, cellular, peripheral nervous system, central nervous system, hormonal, chemical, homeostatic, muscular, emotional, cognitive, linguistic, and on and on.

As we grow up, experience our lives, and draw conclusions, we accumulate these survival instructions, what I am calling retroperceptions, and seamlessly integrate them into the flow of our present experience. They become the ideas of ourselves and our world, from which we continue to experience. In this sense they are unconscious or not visible to us, because they are the ground on which we stand, the lens through which we see, the face we have learned to assume in order to survive.

Just as an eye cannot see itself, our own conclusions about ourselves cannot be seen, are unconscious to us. As long as we want to continue to experience from the position of who we think we are, our "unconscious will arise" whenever the ideas we hold about ourselves are challenged.

This concept of the unconscious, as an integrated body of retroperceptions through which we view ourselves and the world, offers not only a precise and parsimonious explanation of Freud's unconscious, but also the possibility, through modalities like PsychoNoetics, of restructuring it *consciously.*

Suffering and pain as information

Humans have always strived to escape pain. Yet, the ability to feel pain, like the ability to feel pleasure, is necessary for survival and even more, for evolution. At its most basic, pain, like pleasure, is just information. It tells us that something we are doing or something that is happening to us is not in our interest. It teaches us what to stop and what to avoid.

Buddhism teaches that life is suffering but that suffering is not inevitable; we can do something about it. But what do the Buddhists mean by the pain of suffering? Do they mean physical pain? We really can't do anything about that. We can alleviate it somewhat, by taking aspirin or something stronger, but we all are going to experience physical pain. Do they mean the emotional pain of failure and the loss of love? The only way not to fail is not to try. The only way to not lose a loved one is not to love. Do they mean the pain of aging? The only way to avoid that is to die young. Do they mean the pain of not entirely fulfilling our destiny? The only way to avoid that pain is not to be open to our destiny in the first place!

So what do they mean; what is this suffering that is avoidable? It is that part of life's suffering that *we bring upon ourselves!* It is the pain that comes into being as a by-product of the *reality* that we construct. It is the by-product of the difference between our inner, unconscious reality and what is really happening.

If pain and pleasure are fundamentally just *information* to guide our individual efforts to survive and thrive, as well as humanity's efforts to evolve, then pain is telling us something, and we should not *indiscriminately try to escape* it, just as we should not indiscriminately pursue pleasure. So what is the right way to deal with pain and the fear of pain? What is the conscious way? What is the psychonoetic way?

It is to use pain as a signal. Not as a signal to take an aspirin or tranquilizer, not as a signal to defend ourselves, not even as a signal to look at what we are doing wrong, but more as a signal to *reevaluate the reality that we have constructed* for ourselves. For it may be that it is not what we are doing that is wrong, but our self-created reality that is wrong! For whenever we feel pain, it is an indication that our subjective reality is at odds with the greater reality! This is, of course, what the technology of PsychoNoetics aims to correct.

Defensiveness as information about the unconscious

We are used to thinking about ourselves as our conscious minds, while that which we are *unconsciously* occupies a curiously ambiguous position. Sometimes it is us, and sometimes it is not. Although not a hard and fast rule, one of the ways we commonly decide whether our unconscious aspects are us or not is whether we like them. Positive attributes like intelligence are us, while "negative" attributes like shyness or an uncontrollable temper, are not us but someone that we are forced to associate with. (This is the most common situation;

however, some of us are so demoralized that we identify with our negative attributes.)

Much of our reactivity comes about because our conscious mind likes to identify itself with our positive attributes, while our unconscious mind dwells on their negative counterparts. I might be very successful and pride myself as a teacher, but instead of resting secure in my role, I find myself defensive and irritated when someone offers a constructive criticism. My unconscious identifies with an inadequacy that my conscious mind will not admit. Only the defensiveness that I feel and the involuntary whine in my voice offer me a clue that I see myself differently unconsciously than I do consciously.

In order to successfully apply PsychoNoetics to our lives, we first have to stop thinking about ourselves as our *conscious* minds and start thinking about ourselves as a *whole system, of which the greater part is unconscious.* The unconscious part is us, as much and perhaps even more than the conscious part. What's more, this unconscious part is at least equally responsible for our emotions, our actions, and the functioning of our body. In fact unconscious and conscious, negativity and positivity, are polarities; neither of them could exist without the other.

If we take this attitude, if we own both our unconscious parts and our conscious ones, both our negative thoughts and feelings and our positive ones, then it becomes natural to *consciously correct* them all, to bring all aspects of our being in line with present reality.

More and more, we realize that our psyche is not a blank slate. Our past ideas about our world and ourselves reside within us and continually affect how we see our present world. Sometimes this is advantageous, but other times we need to deconstruct whatever ideas we are holding so that we can change our reactions to be appropriate to our present life and world. Clearing is a way of *unlearning* so that we can make way for the new. PsychoNoetics is selective and intentional unlearning. We need to add it to our repertoire of adaptive strategies if we are going to continue to thrive as a race.

Chapter 19
Unlearning for an Evolving World

The human pattern is to resist change within each generation

Anthropology tells us that, despite the human ability to adapt, change in human societies is not easy. Tribal and agrarian societies are wedded to traditions and traditional technologies. Although every generation brings fresh perspectives, the young are carefully taught to do things the way their fathers and grandfathers did, and there are even social mechanisms in place to discourage non-conformity and innovation.

Modern urban societies are marked by technological change, but even here, norms and cultural habits are hard to shift. Older generations especially seem fixed in their ways and unable to participate in up-and-coming trends. In this regard, it's interesting to note that social revolutions generally depend on the participation of the young, the next maturing generation, to breakdown the old social order, the old institutions of church, school, and even family.

The evolutionary learning strategy we have inherited is geared to stasis, to the continuity of existing physical, social, and cultural systems. Sudden, discontinuous, or rapid changes are difficult to manage when our unconscious processes keep us perceiving through the eyes of the past. If a present event is seen through the filter of a past conclusion (even if the past conclusion no longer applies), the event will be misinterpreted, and the response to it will be counter-productive. 'Living in and building on the past' will cease to be an advantage and become an impediment.

The rapidly changing world of today

When I was growing up, mathematics was done on paper. Neatness, a firm grasp of the times tables, and knowing how to do long division and square roots with pencil and paper were emphasized. When I went to graduate school, we had to master a slide rule and a mechanical calculator. Carefulness and accuracy of calculation were important.

Now things are done on a computer. The students who mastered neatness, their times-tables, or the art of careful computation on the mechanical calculator and slide rule don't have a lot to show for their effort. Now, the students who are predisposed to work with computers have the advantage.

Change has become so rapid that the natural turn-over of the generations is insufficient opportunity to evolve society appropriately. The young find themselves being taught old knowledge, even as new understandings are emerging daily that are well-beyond our old textbooks.

On the other hand, some learned categories continue to be relevant and invaluable contexts. Automatically and unconsciously constructing our visual field, as well as seeing, talking, driving, etc., are the nuts and bolts of our daily functioning. These are all learned categories that fulfill the expectation that present circumstances will be more or less the same as those experienced in the past, and unconscious responses will be adaptive ones.

Deciding what to change

The modern world is full of the sorts of discontinuities and reversals that make natural learning counter-productive and at times calamitous. At the same time, some patterns are absolutely vital for human functioning. Although deciding what to change may seem obvious on a technological level, increasingly our decisions are becoming psychological, as we face all of the internal obstacles that prevent us from being present with the current explosion of technology and change.

Consider some examples. For instance, when we are children, we are relatively powerless and taught to yield to adult authority. When we become adults, however, feeling powerless and acting subservient (to authorities) can be an enormous problem. These feelings may lead to an inability to assertively participate in arenas of power.

When the soldier who was injured by shelling is sent back to the battlefield, throwing himself on the ground at the whistle of artillery is adaptive. But the vet who throws himself on the New York City pavement when a bus backfires has got a problem! We call this a psychological problem and give it a classification, post-traumatic stress syndrome, which effectively removes the vet from participating in the world as it is.

When we understand that the foundation of our unconscious learning, our associations of retroperceptions, are amenable to selective change, we will find ourselves powerfully set to adapt to the fluid conditions of our present world.

Our unconscious learning strategy

. More than any of the species, what we humans use to survive is learned, and this learning is governed by an evolutionary survival strategy. Furthermore, whether inherited or learned, the instructions all follow the same strategy, the same guiding assumptions of the unconscious, which are:

1. That what was true for us once will more or less continue to be true.
2. What was true about the world will more or less continue to be true.
3. That both these assumptions are the bedrock on which to build our present perceptions.

The system works well for us as long as these assumptions hold, but breaks down when these assumptions break down! This is as true for us individually as it is for the species as a whole.

Each of us has learned and constructed our unconscious reality as an intervening variable between the world and ourselves, with the assumption that everything will pretty much stay the way it is. In acting as a perceptual filter or interpreter, this "learning" assigns meaning to our experiences and behaviors. In addition, as much as it is an instruction manual, it also contains directives for how to react to the meanings it assigns.

When the assumption holds true that reality is the same in the present as it was in the past, the instructions remain valid and all goes well. But when the world, or our relationship to it, has changed faster than the instruction manual, our expectations of reality comes into conflict with the present, and the inevitable outcome is threat, discord, chaos, dysfunction, ill health, and pain.

This learning strategy has been wildly successful in times of gradual evolution. But at the present, when things are changing at dizzying speed, the world is not the same from one moment to the next, and norms of relationship seem to shift just as quickly, this strategy has broken down completely. It urgently needs to be updated, but there is not sufficient time for the species to evolve a new neurological learning strategy genetically, at least not without a probable large-scale die-off of humanity and perhaps the planet. So we have to evolve on a cultural, technological, and behavioral level instead!

Adaptive overlays

The best that cumulative "natural learning" can offer us in order to adapt to discontinuous situations is an *overlay*. That is, we may overlay one response with another, one which inhibits or redirects it.

At best overlays are cumbersome, at worst, crippling. Consider someone who learns a second language late in life. They continue to think in their first language and then translate to the second, not only finding equivalent words, but even modifying the syntax. The result is laborious, slow, and frequently filled with mistakes. Speech is somewhat adequate for relaxed situations, but in emergency situations where quickness of response, presence of mind, and accuracy of communication are essential, the whole translation process can break down.

Conscious unlearning: A new survival strategy

Devising a new survival strategy has to start by reversing the old, guiding assumption that something once learned to be true is held to be true forever. It has to start with a means of *unlearning*, wiping clean the slate of the unconscious, resetting the bio-computer. This, of course, is what the technology of PsychoNoetics offers.

Psychonoetic protocols first zero in on the maladaptive retroperceptions that falsify our present perceptions, and second, allow us to unlearn them. In this way we correct the contents of our unconscious minds so that they can better serve us in the future.

As we individuals *learn how to unlearn*, we can begin to participate in our societies in more holistic ways, with less suffering and with less defensiveness. As our favorite ideas about ourselves yield to a more authentic presence of being. we come to appreciate the diversity of perspectives that we collectively are as a species, without negative self-reference. And this acceptance, in turn, opens the door to cooperation, collaboration and hopefully survival.

Unlearning the lessons of childhood for the good of our world

One of the most significant changes that absolutely everyone goes through, the change that changes everything, is simply *growing up*. Many of the dramatic and even traumatic lessons of childhood cease to apply in adulthood, and many are strongly counter-indicated.

Where as children we were relatively weak, dependent, and lacking in autonomy, we are now relatively strong, independent, and autonomous. The things that overwhelmed us in childhood should be easily handled as adults. However, if we *retroperceptively* experience our adulthood from our childhood, we will always be stuck in childish perceptions, emotions, and reactions, and we will never come into our full power.

Formative childhood memories come in all varieties, big and small. There are thousands of on-going situations which are challenging, difficult or even traumatic, including rejections, sicknesses, run-ins with authority figures, embarrassments, asserting ourselves, trust betrayed, and love rejected or withdrawn. When the lesson learned in the past continues to be valid, there is no problem; there's just additional learning, as the box of experiences into which we put the present experience continues to fill.

However, this is rarely the case with childhood. When things change radically, when the lessons learned in childhood no longer apply in adulthood, a problem arises. Sometimes it is very big problem, causing confusion and misunderstanding. When this is so, our natural system of associative learning is inadequate and relationships fall apart, divisiveness occurs within organizations, and even nations find themselves acting like children!

A new learning strategy or a corrective for the existing one has to emerge, and there is not enough time to evolve it genetically. We have to take matters in our hands, and create a new strategy in our individual consciousnesses, which can then enter into the collective consciousness!

This corrective strategy has to be a means of *detecting and unlearning* retroperceptions when they cease to be valid and useful. PsychoNoetics is such a corrective. It is essential that it, or something like it, enter the consciousness of the human race, if we are to adapt to our fast changing reality quickly enough to avert an evolutionary die-off.

Chapter 20
The Self-Illuminated Human

Throughout human history, individuals and groups with awakening consciousnesses have been striving to break the code of the unconscious, to gain access to the locked programs of their unconscious minds and revise them, in other words - to take *conscious* control of their psychospiritual evolution.

The three great "consciousness-raising"traditions of the world, psychology, mysticism, and religion, have always been about this to some degree, however unconsciously and unwittingly. In the psychological tradition, this is part of the aim of psychotherapy, hypnosis, and psychoactive drugs. In the mystical tradition this is part of the aim of meditation and yoga. In the religious traditions, this is part of the connection with God. In this regard, PsychoNoetics and to an extent, other "clearing strategies" do not stand alone. They are recent efforts in a great lineage of awakening that will continue to evolve as long as humanity continues to evolve.

PsychoNoetics as a conscious, evolutionary tool

In as much as it breaks the code of the unconscious, PsychoNoetics is a revolutionary transformational paradigm in this great lineage of awakening. The, "technical" aspects of this new paradigm are auto-kinesiological diagnosis, and the clearing strategy itself. But utilizing these techniques with a sacred intention, rather than merely a medical or psychotherapeutic one, qualifies PsychoNoetics to stand as a (clearing) path, alongside the (meditative, devotional, inquiring and psychophysical) paths of Buddhism, Vedanta, Sufism, Gnostic Christianity, Kabbalah, and various, non-traditional spiritual teachings.

Psychonoetic clearing proceeds entirely as a conscious decision to let go. There are no principles to be learned, no identity to be assumed, no examples to be lived up to, no information or teachings to digest. All you need to do to access your real identity as pure consciousness is to understand that *you are That,* and to clear away the memories, thoughts, and feelings that are obstacles to that realization.

Noetic psychologist Allan Combs distinguishes between anabolic and catabolic spiritual paths. Anabolic paths essentially consist of creating or constructing a new state of consciousness (as in affirmations, visualizations, and guided meditations). Catabolic paths, on the other hand, consist of deconstructing customary or habitual states of consciousness and their contents, so that new levels of organization can spontaneously manifest themselves.

PsychoNoetics, intended as a Clearing Path, is catabolic, a path of deconstruction, (although it can be used to guide anabolic processes like affirmations as well). It frees us from illusion and facilitates the acceptance of the reality of *What Is.* True spirituality *can only* emerge from this acceptance.

A fundamental, philosophical division

PsychoNoetics heralds a turn in philosophic orientation for the entirety of Western society. Remember the questions that I posed earlier in the book? Why is it that science, experts, and external authorities have taken such a hold of us, and why are some of us rebelling against this? In previous chapters I have pointed the finger at some of our beliefs about reality, but another part of the answer lies with our unexamined philosophy. Consider this.

There is a fundamental philosophical division in the world, one with widespread moral and ethical implications, which unconsciously influences most of the helping professions that have a "psychological" basis, like education, religion, psychotherapy, and social work. They even influence our legal system. On one side of this divide, people believe in laws and systems of ethical and moral directives. In the west this is exemplified by the Judeo-Christian tradition and in the east by Confucianism. The existence of these directives on how to live an upright life, how to be a good person in society, come out of a belief we have to be told, be taught, and tell ourselves what to do and how to live. This could be characterized as the doctrine of the child human, the human who is perpetually in need of a parent or a parental society.

On the other side of this divide, people believe that all humanity possesses an essential state of being, which it is our mission to uncover and perfect throughout our lives. From this perfected state, wisdom and compassion in thought and action spontaneously emanate. This doctrine is exemplified in the East by the traditions of Taoism, Advaita, and Chan and Zen Buddhism. It could be exemplified in the esoteric reaches of the Judeo-Christian tradition as a state of grace.

This split is not often commented on, but I think it is the most central division in human thought and certainly the division most relevant to the conduct of our lives. It is the difference between being treated or treating ourselves as a child, on the one hand, and being treated or treating ourselves as an adult, on the other. I don't mean an adult plodding beneath the weight of obligations and responsibilities, but a mature being animated and illuminated by an inner light, an inner wisdom, an inner connection to "God".

Where we are

People who have been brought up to believe that man is driven by directives tend to be authoritarian personalities, (i.e., polarly position themselves either in authority or subject to authority) and reify facts and directives. What is more, they do unto others as they do unto themselves, and they do unto themselves as they do unto others. That is, they direct themselves through beliefs, laws, and "shoulds" and, when they have the chance, they impose these "shoulds" upon all others who have the misfortune of coming under their authority: spouses, children, parishioners, employees, or subjects.

Institutions, whether they are governments, religions, armies, or businesses, are even guiltier of this than are individuals. Organized religions, almost without exception, have been the most flagrant abusers and *beneficiaries* of this pernicious tradition. This is a mindset that imprisons mankind.

On the other hand, people who believe that man can be driven by an inner light, a gradually revealed connection to some source of inner wisdom, love, and truth, are inherently as free as their authoritarian counterparts are in bondage.

Most of what passes for education, religious instruction, knowledge, and government by laws, etc., is driven by facts and directives. In some ways science has provided an even more convincing rationale for external directives than the existence of an authoritarian God. There are only a small minority of individuals, philosophies, and institutions who dissent, who are free from this most oppressive delusion.

Envisioning a self-illuminated humanity

We need to firmly ground an alternative body of thought and action on the vision of the *self-illuminated human*. Science, education, government, morality, and ethics, have not only to be recast in this light, but also reconceived in it. People for whom this viewpoint is natural, artists, poets, musicians, visionaries, free spirits and, of course, – *mystics,* must give up their roles as dissenters on the periphery of a bounded society. Instead, they need to come together in mutual affirmation to form an alternate core, a core of inner authority, a core of light, a core society to which people can come as they liberate themselves from authoritarianism. They must recreate our institutions, particularly our schools and churches, in this vision so as to create alternatives for our society and a starting point for our children.

The Clearing Path of PsychoNoetics is aligned with this vision of the self-illuminated human, and is, in fact, facilitating this vision. Learning, information, affirmation, no matter how true and how wise, even learning about the self-illuminated human, are not enough. Only by letting go of everything that we hold on to in the space that is our consciousness, can we come to our real identity, and realize our inner authority.

Enlightened self-interest

We are in a new age, a global ecology where everything and everyone is *visibly* interdependent with everything and everyone else, and where almost all information is a mouse-click away. In this total information environment we are fast realizing that our survival is dependent upon sustaining the global system that sustains us. We are realizing that humanity must put their individual differences and individual identities aside and cooperate towards common goals. For that, we need a higher consciousness, one that sees that our individual interests are inseparable from the interests of the whole. This is no more and no less than *enlightened self-interest*, a new Golden rule that says *do onto the All as you would do onto yourself.*

How can the Clearing Path of PsychoNoetics help bring forth this new realization? We can, of course, be educated to this viewpoint, and a certain amount of education is in order. In fact, it is essential. However, education alone will not shift our consciousness. There is within every one of us an inherited resistance, which, as I have said, derives from our inescapable *identification* with our physical body and its survival. Identification with our body, inclines us towards an equally vulnerable and separated identification with our self-image.

This fundamental, survival urge drives most *competitive* human behavior. It is an evolutionary heritage that must be overcome or at least put into perspective, in order for new patterns of human response-ability to emerge. Clearing practices loosen our identity with our bodies and deconstruct all of the "false" identities that are built upon that. This, in turn, can break down those boundaries that keep humanity at odds with one another. If we envision what a society might be like when this becomes a reality, and our deep interdependency becomes apparent, we will be inspired to follow a clearing path not only for ourselves, but also for all humankind.

The choice

Our lives, however we live them, will always change the outcome, will always influence the evolution of consciousness for better or for worse. If we let ourselves be blind, if we forget who and what we are, our lives will only contribute to the noise and chaos around us and not much good will come out of them. But if we remember, if we take responsibility, if we play hard and true, God Himself will notice and will gladly scoot over on the bench to make room for a new teammate.

Jeff Eisen
Santa Barbara, California
January 1, 2006, The New Year

OMNIUS

The *Clearing Path of PsychoNoetics* is one of the practices of a transformational psychology and philosophy called *Omnius*. Omnius is a call to conscious people of all beliefs to come together in common identity. What is this common identity? It is the universal or God consciousness that we all share, the empty space, the no-thingness that holds equally the contents of every sentient being's mind. To find out more about Omnius and the transformational opportunities it offers, or to contact Dr. Eisen, please go to www.Omnians.com.

Claim the Gift
A postscript by Jeanie DeRousseau Eisen, Ph.D.
AKA Jeanie

Since I play a significant role in the psychonoetic story, Jeff asked me to write something about the story from my perspective. I found myself wanting to somehow convey the creative field that is our family and my gratitude for it. I hope these remarks will serve that purpose.

Jeff and I are in relationship now for almost 19 years. During that time I feel that we have held a steady inner truth and love for one another. At the same time we have friends who wonder at the commitment we have to each other, despite our many differences and the turbulence that comes from these differences.

We have lived in this paradox, miscommunicating, evolving, and co-creating. Our many conversations have been deeply personal and about the biggest pictures of reality. I am very blessed to have experienced Jeff's great gift for exploring the inner spaces of the psychonoetic realm, and my own understandings about human evolution have grown from knowing him. Our daughter Ariel is now a young woman poised on a threshold of awareness and creativity that knocks our socks off. And our hours together are filled with inquiry...

Today, as we walked on a muddy path near Stow Lake, me in my favorite dress boots, Jeff got us a little lost. As I righteously led the way out, I found myself feeling very "I told you so" - so Jeff said, "Will the real Jeanie please come back?" Although I tried (psychonoetically) to clear my righteousness, I couldn't, and instead I replied, "I'm sorry, but I seem to need this energy right now."

When we reached high ground, I also reached a willingness to clear. In doing so, I was struck with the realization that I had been calling upon some energy that I needed in order to assert my intuition about how to proceed. In trying to clear my righteous identity, I was also threatening the confident energy I was drawing upon; I was throwing out the baby with the bath water. What I needed to do, of course, was to recognize the energy and just clear the righteousness, in other words, to *claim the gift*.

After seeing this, Jeff and I started exploring what it meant. We realized that underlying the identities we hold, may be fundamental powers and abilities, and it is often these that keep the identities alive. When we clear, we always want to recognize and claim those aspects, and re-integrate them into *who we are*...

And so it goes with Jeff and I, and hopefully it will be the same with you and your loved ones. We have just begun to explore the inner realms of our experiences. Jeff is an intuitive master of these realms, but they are accessible to us all. In fact, that is the most important part of his teaching. These inner spaces are the next frontier of humanity, where we will come face to face with the nature of who we really are.

Index

213